2004 POETRY

# ONCE UPON A RHYME

## IMAGINATION FOR A NEW GENERATION

# Glasgow Vol II

Edited by Steve Twelvetree

 Young**Writers**

First published in Great Britain in 2004 by:
Young Writers
Remus House
Coltsfoot Drive
Peterborough
PE2 9JX
Telephone: 01733 890066
Website: www.youngwriters.co.uk

SB ISBN 1 84460 495 0

# Foreword

Young Writers was established in 1991 and has been passionately devoted to the promotion of reading and writing in children and young adults ever since. The quest continues today. Young Writers remains as committed to engendering the fostering of burgeoning poetic and literary talent as ever.

This year's Young Writers competition has proven as vibrant and dynamic as ever and we are delighted to present a showcase of the best poetry from across the UK. Each poem has been carefully selected from a wealth of *Once Upon A Rhyme* entries before ultimately being published in this, our twelfth primary school poetry series.

Once again, we have been supremely impressed by the overall high quality of the entries we have received. The imagination, energy and creativity which has gone into each young writer's entry made choosing the best poems a challenging and often difficult but ultimately hugely rewarding task - the general high standard of the work submitted amply vindicating this opportunity to bring their poetry to a larger appreciative audience.

We sincerely hope you are pleased with our final selection and that you will enjoy *Once Upon A Rhyme Glasgow Vol II* for many years to come.

# Contents

| | |
|---|---|
| Dale Henderson  (9) | 17 |
| Michael Curran  (9) | 17 |
| Cameron Boyce  (9) | 18 |
| Justine Green  (9) | 18 |
| Laura Bradshaw  (9) | 18 |

## Barlanark Primary School

| | |
|---|---|
| Andrew Johnstone | 19 |
| Jordan Moffat  (11) | 19 |
| Emma Chastey  (11) | 19 |
| Hayley McFadyen  (8) | 20 |
| James Ferguson  (8) | 20 |
| Tamlyn Stout  (9) | 20 |
| Rebecca Reid  (8) | 21 |
| Shelley Brannigan  (7) | 21 |
| Cheryl Cooper  (9) | 21 |
| Grant Fountain  (9) | 22 |
| Emma Holt  (8) | 22 |
| Gemma McHale  (9) | 22 |
| Scott Campbell  (10) | 23 |
| William Wilson  (11) | 24 |
| Lauren Crooks  (10) | 24 |
| Stephanie Lenehan  (11) | 24 |
| Danielle Patrick  (10) | 25 |
| Jennifer Baillie  (11) | 25 |
| Amanda McQueen  (9) | 26 |
| John McKelvie  (8) | 26 |
| Scott Heap  (11) | 26 |
| Craig Upton  (8) | 27 |
| Karla Deacon  (10) | 27 |
| Ryan Cowan  (11) | 27 |
| Greig Fountain  (11) | 28 |
| Jade Dockrell  (10) | 28 |
| Jason McCarthy  (11) | 28 |
| Kayleigh Scott  (9) | 29 |

## Barrowfield Primary School

| | |
|---|---|
| Jason McArthur  (8) | 29 |
| Nikita Watson  (9) | 30 |
| Jade McKenzie  (8) | 30 |
| Stephen Watson  (8) | 31 |

Miles McCulloch  (9)                         31
Chanel Conor  (8)                            32
Dale Wallace  (9)                            32
Chloe Bruce  (8)                             33
Jacqueline McCrimmon  (8)                    33
Gary Degnan  (9)                             34
Josh McDonald  (9)                           34
Emily Wade  (8)                              35

## Cairns Primary School
Paul Craig  (11)                             35
Lee Marshall  (10)                           35
Glynn Woods  (11)                            36
Chloe Hefferland  (10)                       36
Lauren Johnston  (10)                        37

## Calderwood Primary School
Jonathan Larkins  (7)                        37
Nicola Brown  (7)                            37
Shona Bell  (7)                              38
Morven Bell  (7)                             38
Pamela Blair  (7)                            39
Carly Wilmott  (7)                           39
Ronan Duff  (7)                              39

## Carolside Primary School
Kieran McDonald  (9)                         40
Jennifer Stuart                              40
Stuart McInnes  (9)                          41
Stephen Shindler  (9)                        41
Claire Hamilton  (10)                        42
Stuart Taylor  (10)                          42
Kathryn Wylie  (9)                           43
Lindsay Robertson  (10)                      43
Grant Cairney  (9)                           44
Callum Carmichael  (10)                      44
Sarah Wilson  (9)                            45
Laura Briggs  (9)                            45
Alexander Hannah  (9)                        46
Jacob Hong  (9)                              46
Fraser McDougall  (9)                        46

Jamie Meldrum  (9)                              47
Misha Palmer  (9)                               47
Ailish Ross  (9)                                48
Laura McIntyre  (10)                            48
Andrew Cuthbert  (9)                            49
Douglas Young  (9)                              49
Craig Imrie  (10)                               50
Catriona McCallum  (9)                          50
Calum Husenne  (10)                             51
Robyn Adams  (9)                                51
David MacDonald  (9)                            52
Emma Robertson  (9)                             52
Holly Dryden  (9)                               53
Molly Corcoran  (9)                             53
Sara Kettlewell  (9)                            54
Emma Appleyard  (9)                             54

## Chapelgreen Primary School
Nichola Pinkerton  (10)                         55
Angela Dunbar  (10)                             55
Graeme Marklow  (11)                            56

## Craighead Primary School
Shannon Lawson  (10)                            56
Lorna Reid  (10)                                57
Lisa Main  (10)                                 57
Andrew Quirk  (9)                               58
Suzanne Nicholson  (10)                         58
Laura Dover  (9)                                59

## David Livingstone Memorial Primary School
Calum Ronaldson  (11)                           60
Carly McPhee  (11)                              60
Kirsten Darling  (11)                           61
Ross Burns  (11)                                61
Lauren Munro  (11)                              62
Pamela Heaney  (11)                             62
Monique Bennett  (10)                           63
David Kelly  (11)                               63
Lauren Buddy  (10)                              64
Lauren McKenzie  (11)                           64

| | |
|---|---|
| Erin Dean  (12) | 65 |
| Clare Carruthers  (11) | 65 |
| Natasha Monteith  (10) | 66 |
| Robert Gracie  (11) | 66 |
| Courtney Lanaghan  (10) | 67 |
| Sarah Brozio  (10) | 67 |
| Alysha Sommerville  (10) | 68 |
| Emma Chambers  (10) | 68 |
| Graeme Goodall  (10) | 68 |
| Rachel McKinnon  (10) | 69 |
| James MacGregor  (10) | 69 |
| Steven Clark  (10) | 70 |
| Andrew Murphy  (10) | 70 |
| Stuart Robertson  (10) | 71 |
| Fraser Jamieson  (10) | 71 |
| Laura Neillis  (8) | 72 |
| Scott Henderson  (10) | 72 |
| Leeanne Kennedy  (10) | 73 |
| Alasdair Adams  (10) | 74 |
| Chloe Coventry  (10) | 74 |
| Bradley Inglis  (7) | 74 |
| Derek Whiteford  (10) | 75 |
| Taylor Farrell  (7) | 75 |
| Daryn Smith  (7) | 75 |
| Christopher Irvine  (10) | 76 |
| Scott McCormick  (7) | 76 |
| Keir Johnson  (7) | 76 |
| Andrea Dobbins  (7) | 77 |
| Aimee Kane  (8) | 77 |
| Joseph Steel  (8) | 77 |
| Jamie Balsillie  (8) | 78 |
| Cameron Dean  (7) | 78 |
| Gary Hughes  (8) | 78 |
| Abbey McInulty  (7) | 79 |
| Rachel Irvine  (8) | 79 |
| Jordan McTaggart  (7) | 79 |
| Rachel Darling  (8) | 80 |
| Rebecca Carruthers  (6) | 80 |
| Andrew Hutcheson  (8) | 80 |
| Hollie Tavendale  (7) | 81 |
| Jack Conner  (7) | 81 |

## Glenmanor Primary School

| | |
|---|---|
| Jordan Gallagher  (11) | 81 |
| Craig Berry  (11) | 82 |
| Christopher McGovern  (11) | 83 |
| Nicole Marsland  (10) | 84 |
| Natalie Dyer  (11) | 85 |

## Hillhead Primary School

| | |
|---|---|
| Jamie Horne  (11) | 85 |
| Gregg Boyd  (10) | 86 |
| Kirsty Chalmers  (11) | 86 |

## Our Lady of the Annunciation Primary School

| | |
|---|---|
| Sarah Airlie  (10) | 87 |
| Daniel Squire  (10) | 87 |
| Louise Gregory  (10) | 88 |
| Catriona Jordan  (10) | 88 |
| Max Graham  (10) | 89 |
| Matthew Paterson  (10) | 89 |
| Shannan Wilkie  (10) | 90 |
| Conor Clafferty  (10) | 90 |
| Aidan Russell  (10) | 91 |
| Ross Hannah  (10) | 91 |
| Michael Mullaney  (10) | 92 |
| Roisin Gallacher  (10) | 92 |
| Kathryn Murphy  (10) | 93 |
| Angela Traynor  (10) | 93 |

## St Hilary's Primary School, East Kilbride

| | |
|---|---|
| Louise Reilly & Lewis Howie  (9) | 94 |
| Callum Little  (8) | 94 |
| Emma Anderson  (11) | 95 |
| Mark Edison & Alix Boylett  (8) | 95 |
| Colette Baptie  (10) | 96 |
| David McMonagle & Joshua Cairns  (8) | 96 |
| Matthew Quinn  (9) | 97 |
| Stefano Di Vito  (10) | 97 |
| Simone Reilly  (10) | 98 |
| Vicki Murdoch  (11) | 99 |

| Andrew Moran (10) | 99 |
| Rachel Griffin (11) | 100 |

## St Machan's Primary School, Lennoxtown

| Maria Smith (9) | 100 |
| Andrew Allan (10) | 101 |
| Christian McKenna (9) | 101 |
| Josh Gallagher (10) | 102 |
| Melissa Ingleby (10) | 102 |
| Megan Pickett (10) | 103 |
| Kerry Simpson (9) | 103 |
| Megan Duff (9) | 104 |
| Amy O'Donnell (9) | 104 |
| Fraser MacDonald (9) | 105 |
| Dominic McMahon (9) | 105 |
| John MacDonald (9) | 105 |
| Hannah Sweeney (10) | 106 |
| Megan Griffin (9) | 106 |
| Thomas Rocks (9) | 106 |
| Ryan Wheeler (9) | 107 |
| Anna Turlewicz (9) | 107 |
| Claire McEntee (9) | 107 |
| Michael Harkins (9) | 108 |
| Connor Hughes (9) | 108 |
| Eireanne Ovens (9) | 108 |
| Jordan McElhaney (9) | 109 |
| Gary McGhee (9) | 109 |
| Natalie Young (9) | 109 |
| Elizabeth Carney (9) | 110 |
| Amy Magill (9) | 110 |
| David Mackenzie (9) | 110 |
| Michelle Kearney (9) | 111 |
| Kimberley McLarry (9) | 111 |

## St Peter's Primary School, Partick

| Darren McLean (9) | 111 |
| Megan McMenamin (9) | 112 |
| Michelle McGurn (9) | 113 |
| Ciaran McClymont (9) | 113 |
| Amy Smart (9) | 114 |
| Rachael McDonald (9) | 114 |

# The Poems

# Cats

*(Based on 'Cats Sleep Anywhere' by Eleanor Farjeon)*

Cats sleep
Anywhere,
Beside the fish tank,
Beside the hamster cage,
On the table,
On the chair,
Cats sleep
Anywhere.
They don't care,
Fluffy's not
A lap cat,
But he loves
Felix the cat food,
He's loved Felix food
Since he was a kitten,
Cats sleep anywhere
They don't care.

**Jade Ward (8)**
**Auchenback Primary School**


# Cats

*(Based on 'Cats Sleep Anywhere' by Eleanor Farjeon)*

Cat sleeps anywhere,
On the piano,
On the window ledge,
In an open drawer,
In a cardboard box,
He eats cat biscuits,
He does not open himself,
He says six words,
His name is Victory,
He is 36 months old,
He loves me so much.

**Vicki Addison (8)**
**Auchenback Primary School**

# Cats

My cat lives in a house on a bed,
All she does every day is sleep,
Her name is Sleepy,
When I come in from the shops,
She opens the bag of cat biscuits by herself,
She eats them all in one day and
When she has finished them,
She goes back to sleep,
That is why I like her.

**Katie O'Donnell  (8)**
**Auchenback Primary School**


# Ode To A Dish

Chicken curry
Chicken curry
I won't have enough
I'll just have to eat you all up
I can't get enough
You're just wonderful stuff
You're slippy and sloppy
I just can't get enough.

**David Paterson  (8)**
**Auchenback Primary School**


# Butterfly

Grubby is her name
When she speaks
Every word is the same.
She lives in the garden
On her own,
When she sees something,
She eats it alone.

**Carly Kennedy  (8)**
**Auchenback Primary School**

# Cranky The Octopus

Cranky jumps about when he sees a boat
When it's cold he always has his coat
Cranky eats a lot of things
To become so powerful
When he's finished, it's so dull.

Cranky is thirty-eight and lives in a
Stinking tank in France.
He will speak English
Just when boats come
He'll scoop them in his mouth
Like ice creams.
Cranky lives on his own
But likes to use the telephone.

**George Rennie (8)**
**Auchenback Primary School**


# Ode To A Dish

Pot Noodle, Pot Noodle,
You're wonderful stuff
Slishy, slimy and spicy
I love you a lot
And I think you're so hot
You're greasy and juicy
I love you so much
And I want more
On my plate
More on my plate
You remind me of
Chicken noodle soup
And I love you so much
I can't get enough.

**Morgan Gray (8)**
**Auchenback Primary School**

# Cats

My cat lives in the garden
My cat's called Lady.
She always eats cat biscuits because
They're the best for her.
She's always sleeping on
the window ledge.
She's always in a crabby mood
When she gets up.
You better
Watch out
The garden's a midden.

**Vicki McDougal  (8)**
**Auchenback Primary School**


# My Little Cousin Dillon

He collects Lord of the Rings figures,
Dinosaurs, PlayStation 2 games,
He likes to play the PS2, KFC, Burger King, games, football,
Cars, motorbikes.
He likes dressing up as a pirate, wizard.
He is cool, funny and most important, I like him.

**Emma Paterson  (10)**
**Bankhead Primary School**


# My Big Sister Angela

She collects lots of make-up
Lots of shoes too
And she wears them when they're just new
She buys new clothes
Then she moans she's got nothing to do
But then she goes to the shows
She buys chains, bracelets and earrings.

**Elissa Scott  (10)**
**Bankhead Primary School**

# My Hamster

My hamster
Sleeps
Eats and
Drinks
All day.

My hamster
Is very
Snuggly
And loves
Cuddles.

My hamster
Is not
Vicious or
Fierce
Doesn't bite.

My hamster
Is friendly
It is a Siberian
Hamster.

**Megan Stewart  (9)**
**Bankhead Primary School**


# Hospital

H elen
O ut
S ide
P lays
I n
T he
A nnual
L akes.

**Megan Clark  (9)**
**Bankhead Primary School**

## Acrostic Poems

S pring is
P ast
R ain
I s
N ow waiting
G et ready.

S miling children
U nder the sun
M elting ice cream
M elting everywhere
E ating outside
R iding donkeys.

A utumn
U sually
T urns
U mber
M aple
N ow.

W indy days
I cicles
N ight noises
T elevision
E arly to bed
R ain.

**Declan McGinley (9)**
**Bankhead Primary School**


## Winter

W inter brings the cold weather in
I t's time to put on warm clothes
N ow it gets dark early
T he people wear big jackets
E at your dinner to keep you warm
R emember to keep safe.

**Scott McCaugey (9)**
**Bankhead Primary School**

# What To Find In A Witch's Cauldron

This is what you will find in a witch's cauldron,
Green slime and eyes of bats.

Insects, tails of cats,
Poison and a sizzle and a bang
Shark's tooth and a devil's fang.

Vampire's blood, lion's claw,
Snake skin, dog's paw
Sheep's wool, pig's ear,
Cat's hair, antler of deer.

Slime soup, elephant's trunk,
Horse's hoof, ear of a chipmunk,
Orangatang's arm, gorilla's foot,
Fish's eye, a human's boot.

So don't visit a witch or you must be off your mind,
But if you do visit one that's what you'll find!

**Melissa Crabb  (9)**
**Bankhead Primary School**


# My Wee Cousin

She collects shells and marbles
Insects and spiders
Bits of rock and stone
She is
Annoying
Loud
Messy
Smelly
Dirty
And has staring eyes.

**Nicola Bell  (10)**
**Bankhead Primary School**

## My Mental Cousin

He collects bangers in his house
Maybe there is a little dead mouse.
He always runs away 'cause he wants to go and play.
He's only three years old.
He loves to be in the cold
He is always in a little giggle.
He likes to jump about and jiggle.
He would like to knock down a tower.
He hates sweets that are sour
He jumps over the gate
To get his friend that's eight.
He hates to be in the dark
Guess what? His name is Mark.
He's always been mental and crazy
Since he was a little baby.

**Jamie-Lee Turner  (10)**
**Bankhead Primary School**


## My Little Brother

My little brother is mental and crazy
Ever since he was a little baby
He collects toilet roll holders
Feathers and rocks
He's always drawing little clocks.

He collects worms that wriggle
He's always in a little giggle
He loves ice cream
He collects insects in a jar
And wants a big blue guitar.

**Alison Hill  (10)**
**Bankhead Primary School**

# What You Would Find In A Witch's House

Two days ago I went to a witch's house
I found a cauldron
Two shelves filled with bats' wings and a mouse
Ten people with their heads chopped off,
And a witch's weird warehouse.

I also saw a flying broomstick
Cracked walls, windows and doors,
A spell book with tricks,
And deadly books,
With a wolf's lick.

I found huge knights
And pretend wolves
Models of elephants having fights
That is what you'll find in a witch's house
It'll be scary at night.

**Rachel McLean (9)**
**Bankhead Primary School**

# My Horses

I have two mighty horses
I ride them about the riding courses
One is auburn the other is brown
When I ride them I never frown
I have two mighty horses.

Every day I go up to the stable
I don't have a timetable
I can ride them whenever I want
I don't have to shout or taunt
They just go when I say
'Come on! Come on! Hooray! Hooray!'

I have two pet horses!

**Shannon McEnroy (10)**
**Bankhead Primary School**

# Brother!

He moans all the time,
He's impatient in line,
He jumps about,
He screams and shouts,
He is mean
But when he sees food he's keen.
He burns it off on his trampoline,
He watches TV,
He doesn't like me,
He also plays on his PC.
He sings in the shower,
He's way smaller than a tower,
He acts like he's seven,
But he's really eleven!

**Lisa Kerr  (10)**
**Bankhead Primary School**


# Big Brother

He collects money same as me
PlayStation 2 games
Models of cars like me
Shells from the beach
Stones that are nice
Magazine just like me
Videos fun to watch
Books good to read
Pictures to put on the wall
Supports Rangers
And friends that are good.

**Michael Phillips  (10)**
**Bankhead Primary School**

# My Little Sister

My sister is a monkey
She makes mud pies
Collects stones and pebbles
She acts all shy!

Half-made models
Disgusting things
Kicks herself
Thinks she's so perfect.

She collects stickers
Looks like a clown
Likes to swing on a bed
And has some disgusting friends.

**Rachel Magee  (9)**
**Bankhead Primary School**


# My Wee Brother

He gets really muddy
He has a really great buddy
Even though he's in a hurry
He likes chicken curry
Even though he acts like Murray
Then he is really furry
He acts like a purry
But he's really funny
He even goes to nursery
At Bankhead Primary
After it he's really sleepy
At night he is really creepy.

**Thomas Graham  (10)**
**Bankhead Primary School**

# Seasons Acrostic Poem

S pring
P ears
R ise
I n
N ice
G ardens

S un
U ses
M ore
M etal
E verywhere
R ound

A ll
U gly
T rees
U se
M otion
N otices

W ater
I cicle
N ipping
T ongues
E ars
R obbers

**Lauren MacDonald (9)**
**Bankhead Primary School**


# Elephant Haiku

Elephants walk slow
They like to have a big bath
Elephants have trunks.

**Dylan Ewart (9)**
**Bankhead Primary School**

# My Mate Mikey

I like Mikey
Because he is big and spikey
He likes to eat
Lots and lots of meat
He likes to sit on a seat
Playing his Gameboy without a cheat
I liked him ever since
And he eats a lot of mince
He can climb a fence
And he saves up fifty pence.

**Daniel Carlton (10)**
**Bankhead Primary School**


# Why Calum Is My Best Mate

Calum is my best mate because he is a Rangers fan,
He also likes noodles made in a pan,
He likes a KFC just the same as he likes me,
He always likes to make things but would never wear rings,
Calum is funny and he's mental but would always be gentle.

PS - All be wary because he can be scary.

**Craig Anderson (10)**
**Bankhead Primary School**


# Books

A book is a place
Just open it up and step in
Lost kingdoms with magic keys
You can sail seven seas
Climb snowy mountains
Fly to the moon
Swim with whales
Whenever you wish.

**Marc Butler (9)**
**Bankhead Primary School**

# My Dog

I love my dog because she's a part of my family too.
So here's a list of what she likes to do.
My dog is very small,
Though she loves to play with her ball,
Any shape, any size,
But when she bites it, it starts to minimise.

We play about all the time,
We even like to make up pantomimes,
But when she accidentally bites my hand,
We have to rush to hospital (or as I call it, Misery Land).
The doctors finally fix it,
I don't give her a bone, but only doggy biscuits.

She pulls and tangles all the blankets out of her bed,
Then my gran has to give her a smack on the head.
I mostly love to play with her outside,
But sometimes she gets over the boundary of excite,
But when she really starts to bark,
It's when we're out having fun at the park.

**Lauren McGugan (9)**
**Bankhead Primary School**


# My Best Friend

I don't have a best friend,
But if I did it would be Jamie-Lee
Her nickname is Jama,
She has brown hair,
Green eyes and
Always wears plaits.
She's quite tall
And really slim.
She's never ever in a dim.
That's definitely Jama!

**Kaitlin Cross (10)**
**Bankhead Primary School**

# Why Craig's My Best Mate

Craig's my best mate because,
He's a Rangers fan just like me.
He likes to have a kick about in and out the goals,
He likes a KFC as much as he likes me.
He likes The Simpsons just like me.
He likes the PS2 as much as I do.
He likes to have a carry on same as me.
He likes to fight with swords and sticks.
He likes to watch the TV.
He likes to collect ants.
That is why he's my best mate.

PS - He is as dodgy as me!

**Calum Dow  (10)**
**Bankhead Primary School**


# A New Friend

That's me at swimming,
There's a girl that I met,
She has a little sister
And a really cool pet.

I stayed at her house last night,
And I somehow hurt my leg,
Her little sister ran in,
And hit me with an egg.

When I got up this morning,
I played with my ball
I slipped on some juice
And landed on her doll.

**Morgan McKinnon  (9)**
**Bankhead Primary School**

# My Dog

My dog
Is
Friendly
Fierce
And
Very
Fast.
My dog
Barks
And
Doesn't
Like
Sharks.

**Jack Hair (9)**
**Bankhead Primary School**


# Books

A book is a place
Climb snowy mountains
Swim with whales
Just open a book and step in
You can sail seven seas
Fly to the moon
Speak with ghosts
Hear mermaids croon.

**Ryan Bennett (9)**
**Bankhead Primary School**


# Haiku - Sweets

Sweets are nice and smooth
Sweets can be sweet and yummy
Sweeties are the best.

**Megan O'Brien (9)**
**Bankhead Primary School**

## Acrostic Poem

S pring
P uts
R oses
I n
N ice
G ardens.

S ummer
U sually
M akes
M e
E ntirely
R ed.

A nthony
U sually
T akes
U p
M ore
N esting.

W inter
I s
N ippy
T o
E ars
R udely.

**Dale Henderson  (9)**
**Bankhead Primary School**

## Monsters And Giants

There once was a giant called Hairy
People thought he was scary.

When he went to bed
He bumped his head
And he ended up as a fairy.

**Michael Curran  (9)**
**Bankhead Primary School**

# My Dog

My dog
Is barking
Mad.
He's wild
As wild
Can be.

When my
Dog sheds
His hair
It is like a
Summer fair.

**Cameron Boyce  (9)**
**Bankhead Primary School**


# School's Out

That's me Justine
In school doing a test
I think and think
And tried to do my best.

That's me again
Climbing up a tree
I fall off
And break my knee.

**Justine Green  (9)**
**Bankhead Primary School**


# Haiku Animals

I love animals
Animals love to be loved
Pets are the best things.

**Laura Bradshaw  (9)**
**Bankhead Primary School**

# The Spook Song

In a trunk,
In a haunted trunk,

In an attic
In a haunted attic,

In a house,
In a haunted house,

In a wood,
In a haunted wood,

In a bed,
In your bed,

Now I feel safe and loved.

**Andrew Johnstone**
**Barlanark Primary School**


# A Christmas Poem

Christmas,
Lovely tree,
Presents for all,
Fun all around us,
Children having fun opening presents,
Great fun.

**Jordan Moffat (11)**
**Barlanark Primary School**


# Roses

Roses,
Sweet roses,
Lovely smelling roses,
Soft, silky, lovely petals,
Sweet smelling roses for evermore,
Beautiful roses.

**Emma Chastey (11)**
**Barlanark Primary School**

# The Daffodil

My daffodil is pretty.

The daffodil feels cuddly.

My daffodil is feeling warm
Because the spring is coming.

Today my daffodil is soft.

When I see my daffodil I feel happy
Because it is always smiling.

**Hayley McFadyen  (8)**
**Barlanark Primary School**


# The Daffodil

My daffodil is beautiful.
It feels smooth.

My daffodil is feeling mysterious
Because I don't know what it is feeling.

Today my daffodil is as pleased as punch.

When I see my daffodil I feel happy
Because it is smiling.

**James Ferguson  (8)**
**Barlanark Primary School**


# My Favourite Colour

My favourite colour is lilac,
It gives me good luck,
I love to wear my lilac top
And lilac bobble in my hair,
And I see in my dreams
A lilac bear!

**Tamlyn Stout  (9)**
**Barlanark Primary School**

# The Daffodil

My daffodil is warm.

My daffodil feels soft.

My daffodil is feeling happy
Because it is sunny.

Today my daffodil is lonely.

When I see my daffodil I feel happy
Because it is always smiling at me.

**Rebecca Reid  (8)**
**Barlanark Primary School**


# The Daffodil

My daffodil is happy.

It feels excited.

My daffodil is feeling glad
Because it is her birthday.

Today my daffodil is cuddly.

When I see my daffodil I feel happy
Because it is happy too.

**Shelley Brannigan  (7)**
**Barlanark Primary School**


# My Niece

When I get my photo taken
I get one with my niece
She wriggles and wriggles
And jiggles and jiggles
And nobody knows but me.

**Cheryl Cooper  (9)**
**Barlanark Primary School**

# Moany Mum

My mum is very moany
She moans every day
Everytime she moans
We always kick her toes
She says she moans
Because we're noisy boys
We think we're only having fun
But sometimes I think we
Annoy our mum!

**Grant Fountain  (9)**
**Barlanark Primary School**


# The Daffodil

My daffodil is wonderful.

The yellow flower feels bright.

My daffodil is feeling happy
Because it is not lonely.

Today my daffodil is friendly.

When I see my daffodil I feel nice
Because it is cute.

**Emma Holt  (8)**
**Barlanark Primary School**


# Colours

My favourite colour is purple
I like it very much
I like to see the purple flowers
I like to lick a purple lolly
And cuddle my purple dolly.

**Gemma McHale  (9)**
**Barlanark Primary School**

# TV

TV, television, it's all the same
It's the same but not lame
I am so glad there is a TV
If there wasn't I just wouldn't be me.
TV is so fun, it's great
It's even my best mate.
I watch TV when I'm eating my food
I do that because it's so good.
You can watch football, wildlife and crime.
TV yes, it's just fine.
I get home from school, TV's on - yes!
I lie there in my own mess.
If I came home and TV wasn't there
I would turn into an angry bear.
On TV anything can happen
I don't even move when the door is chappin'
In school no TV, it's just hell.
I love it when I hear the home time bell.
You need a TV to play a PlayStation.
I would even watch TV on vacation.
It's great just to watch my football team score.
I always watch more and more.
Sometimes I watch the news,
TV shows you great beautiful views.
I would love to get my face on TV
So I could shout out 'That's me!'
I hate it when I have to go to bed
I hate it because I am TV in the head.
I love TV so much I took the time,
I took the time to make this rhyme.

**Scott Campbell  (10)**
**Barlanark Primary School**

# Poetry

Poetry can be funny,
Or it can be sad.
Every time you finish one,
You will feel quite glad.
Two or three a night is good.
Read other people's too.
They will keep you happy,
In a very good mood
You know it is fun to read poems.

**William Wilson  (11)**
**Barlanark Primary School**


# Love Poem

Love, love is so romantic you can see it in your eyes
And even when you smile you can see your big brown eyes
Love is like a life and you only have one
When you give everything up for just that one
And when you break up and you have nothing left
You'll be homeless and poor but it's really up to you
So think about it
It's your life.

**Lauren Crooks  (10)**
**Barlanark Primary School**


# Over The Hills And Far Away

Lovely, smiling faces from happy children.
Over the hills and far away,
All the children like to play.
Vanilla cones on a hot sunny day.
Everyone likes to play.
Over the hills and far away.

**Stephanie Lenehan  (11)**
**Barlanark Primary School**

# About My Dad

I love it when you're around
Because I know you really care
When I come to think of you
You are my big brown bear.

My dad is short and stocky
And he is very smart
He loves the film Rocky
And has a great big heart.

My dad loves to irritate
I hate when he irritates me
He never tries to concentrate
He is a Barry Ferguson wannabe.

**Danielle Patrick  (10)**
**Barlanark Primary School**


# Eczema Poem

It really hurts
even a small touch.

My hands are rough
but I'll be tough.

My hands really itch,
I'm like a witch.

My hands are in pain,
like they've been squashed by a
chain.

It's like I've been cut with a knife,
but I get on with my life.

**Jennifer Baillie  (11)**
**Barlanark Primary School**

# The Daffodil

My daffodil is quiet.

My daffodil feels soft.

My daffodil is feeling happy
Because it is sunny.

Today my daffodil is cool.

When I see my daffodil I feel wonderful
Because it is wonderful too.

**Amanda McQueen  (9)**
**Barlanark Primary School**


# The Daffodil

My daffodil is sweet.

The flower feels gorgeous.

My daffodil is feeling cool
Because it is cuddly.

Today my flower is sad.

When I see my daffodil I feel unhappy
Because its head is down.

**John McKelvie  (8)**
**Barlanark Primary School**


# A Winter Day

P eople playing in the snow
O ut in the fresh air
E xcited as the snow falls
M y last snowball.

**Scott Heap  (11)**
**Barlanark Primary School**

# The Daffodil

My daffodil is yellow.
My daffodil feels happy.
My daffodil is feeling cool
Because it is golden.
Today my daffodil is tall.
When I see my daffodil I feel cuddly
Because it is good.

**Craig Upton  (8)**
**Barlanark Primary School**


# Playing In The Park

P ushing the roundabout for my friends.
O ver the grass, playing tig.
E ating at the picnic.
T elling my friends jokes.
R unning around the park playing
   hide-and-seek.
Y oung children sliding down the chute.

**Karla Deacon  (10)**
**Barlanark Primary School**


# Valentine

P als forever
A rose for you
L ove in the air
S how that you like them.

**Ryan Cowan  (11)**
**Barlanark Primary School**

# Poetry

P oems are cool,
O n the way to school.
E veryone likes them.
T here's sad and mad,
R ather glad.
Y ou'll soon like them too.

**Greig Fountain (11)**
**Barlanark Primary School**


# Holidays

H olidays are fun
O f course they are!
L ying on the beach
I n the sun having fun
D ays are flying by,
A week passed already.
Y ummy ice cream.

**Jade Dockrell (10)**
**Barlanark Primary School**


# Seaside

P laying is fun,
O n and off the sandy beach,
E very day, lying beside the pool side.
T rotting along the seaside.
R unning straight through the salty water.
Y oung and old enjoying the sun.

**Jason McCarthy (11)**
**Barlanark Primary School**

# My Jumper

My jumper is pink
My jumper is blue
My jumper is every colour of the rainbow
I love to wear my coloured jumper
Because it makes me feel warm and cosy
I wear it on a Saturday
When I visit my gran.

**Kayleigh Scott (9)**
**Barlanark Primary School**


# Chimpanzees

Chimpanzees, there are ten
One killed a hen.

Chimpanzees, there are nine
One saw a sign.

Chimpanzees, there are eight
One made a mate.

Chimpanzees, there are seven
One went to Heaven.

Chimpanzees, there are six
One always kicks.

Chimpanzees, there are five
One took a dive.

Chimpanzees, there are four
One was on the floor.

Chimpanzees, there are three
One drowned in the sea.

Chimpanzees, there are two
One went to Hong Kong Phooie.

Chimpanzees, there is one
They all had good fun.

**Jason McArthur (8)**
**Barrowfield Primary School**

# Ten Little Flowers

Ten little flowers sitting in the grass
One played dead and then there were nine.

Nine little flowers sitting on the grass
One got sunburn and then there were eight.

Eight little flowers sitting in the grass
A man came along and stamped on one and then there were seven.

Seven little flowers sitting in the grass
One got picked and then there were six.

Six little flowers sitting in the grass
One died and then there were five.

Five little flowers sitting in the grass
One melted and then there were four.

Four little flowers sitting in the grass
One went to Heaven and then there were three.

Three little flowers sitting in the grass
One got taken away and then there were two.

Two little flowers sitting in the grass
One ran away and then there was one.

One little flower sitting in the grass
That ran away and then there were none.

**Nikita Watson  (9)**
**Barrowfield Primary School**


# Nonsense Poem

Hiddle diddle dumpling
My mother is a pumpkin
She went to Spain
And broke her vein
And came back like a dumpling!

**Jade McKenzie  (8)**
**Barrowfield Primary School**

# The Writer Of This Poem

*(Based on 'The Writer Of This Poem' by Roger McGough)*

The writer of this poem . . .
Is as wee as can be
As strong as the north wind
As yummy as a pea

As hairy as a bear
As blunt as a pencil
As weak as a little ant
As clear as a window

The writer of this poem . . .
Always ceases to amaze
He's not one in a million billion
Or so the poem says.

**Stephen Watson  (8)**
**Barrowfield Primary School**

# Kangaroo

In Australia lived kangaroos five.
Now one of them is not alive.

In Australia lived kangaroos four.
One was scared by a giant roar.

In Australia lived kangaroos three.
One of them was chased by a bee.

In Australia lived kangaroos two.
One had to go home because he caught the
flu.

In Australia lived kangaroo one.
He was killed by a currant bun.

**Miles McCulloch  (9)**
**Barrowfield Primary School**

# Little Pups

Five little pups sleeping on the floor
One woke up and then there were four.

Four little pups sitting on a tree
One fell off then there were three.

Three little pups wondering what to do
One got the flu then there were two.

Two little pups having lots of fun
One went for a run and now there was one.

One little pup looking at the sun
It went to have some fun, then there were none!

**Chanel Conor  (8)**
**Barrowfield Primary School**


# The Homeless

There is no need to stand and stare
These homeless people need our care.
They sleep outdoors with no electricity or heat
They beg, steal or borrow and also cheat
They will do just about anything to stay on their feet.
The majority are addicts, in some sort of way
They live their lives and hope and pray
That some day they can live in a normal way.
They can go for days without something to eat
A night in a police cell for them is a treat
So let us spare a thought and a prayer
For the homeless people living on our street.

**Dale Wallace  (9)**
**Barrowfield Primary School**

# Little Girls

Five little girls playing on the floor
One went to the USA then there were four.

Four little girls sitting on a tree
One went away and said boo and then there were three.

Three little girls standing on the tree
One went away and then there were two.

Two little girls sitting in the sun
One went boo hoo and then there was one.

One little girl playing in the sun
And then there were none.

**Chloe Bruce  (8)**
**Barrowfield Primary School**


# Five Little Girls

Five little girls sitting on the store
One fell off now there are four.

Four little girls sitting on a tree
One fell off and broke her knee.

Three little girls had the flu
One flew away then there were two.

Two little girls having fun
One ran away now there was one.

One little girl all by herself
She went home and then there were none!

**Jacqueline McCrimmon  (8)**
**Barrowfield Primary School**

# Counting Rhyme

Five little bears climbing some stairs
One fell down and broke his crown.

Four little bears climbing some stairs
One got up and went to bed.

Three little bears climbing some stairs
One fell off and went in a huff.

Two little bears climbing some stairs
One was tired so it ran to bed.

One little bear climbing some stairs
One fell off and said, 'Tough.'
And then there were none.

**Gary Degnan  (9)**
**Barrowfield Primary School**


# Five Little Tigers

Five little tigers sitting on a door
One fell off and then there were four.

Four little tigers sitting on a tree
One fell and broke his knee, then there were three.

Three little tigers sitting on a shoe
One fell off and then there were two.

Two little tigers sitting on a bun
One ran away and then there was one.

One little tiger sitting on his own
He went home and then there were none!

**Josh McDonald  (9)**
**Barrowfield Primary School**

# The Pest

The pest is James he mucks up all my games
For he is my little brother who likes to get into bother
He can be sweet but the best time is when he is asleep
My little brother the pest.

**Emily Wade  (8)**
**Barrowfield Primary School**


# My Little World

My little world is far, far away
Where it stays as bright as day.

My little world is so small
I can't fit in a football.

All I really want is to see my world come true
Then even more people can see it too.

**Paul Craig  (11)**
**Cairns Primary School**


# My Hero

Peter Loven Krands is my hero
Rangers have two and Celtic have zero.
He scores a goal nearly every game
Sometimes he misses, oh what a shame.
I tried to copy him with his hair
But it didn't turn out quite that fair.
He has black boots I have white
He hits a shot the keeper gets a fright.
He is as fast as a cheetah that is what I like
I can't even keep up with him on my bike.

**Lee Marshall  (10)**
**Cairns Primary School**

# My Friends

I have a lot of friends,
They are very kind to me.
When they come to my house,
They have a cup of tea.

When we go out we take the dogs,
Then we go to the park.
We take the dogs for a walk
And we don't go home till dark.

Friends have lots in common
Like mine all like to sing,
But don't annoy them too much,
They don't like everything.

Friends are very useful
They all are the best.
Friends are very helpful
But don't put them to the test.

**Glynn Woods  (11)**
**Cairns Primary School**


# My Pet Rabbit

My pet rabbit
Does lots of things
Like running away
And chewing up my swings.

My pet rabbit
I still can't see
Why she does those things
Like scratching me.

My pet rabbit
Is full of fun
When she plays
With me she is as
Bright as the sun.

**Chloe Hefferland  (10)**
**Cairns Primary School**

# Seasons

Spring is coming hip, hip, hooray
So that means that winter is going away.
How I wish that summer was here.
After spring it will be near.
In autumn all the leaves fall off the trees
And the trees shake in the breeze.

**Lauren Johnston  (10)**
**Cairns Primary School**

# Felix The Cat

He was known as Felix the hunter
And he spent most of his time in a bunter
Like other cats
He was always chasing rats . . .
And sometimes a mouse around the house.

He liked to snare his prey in the dark
Roaming around the local park
One day Felix was found
Due to the result of a hound
He lay there dead on the ground.

**Jonathan Larkins  (7)**
**Calderwood Primary School**

# The Sheep That Ran Away!

There once was a sheep called Tilly,
Who liked to wear dresses all frilly,
She was asked 'Please don't be silly'
But instead ran over the hilly,
She was met by a man who had a good tan,
He said 'Don't be silly get back over the hilly.'

**Nicola Brown  (7)**
**Calderwood Primary School**

# The Big Fat Boy

There once was a boy
Who was terribly fat,
He was really sick,
So he sat on a mat.

His mum and dad called the doctor
The doctor said he would come over soon.
They waited and waited
When the doctor came it was noon.

The doctor said 'Don't eat any sweets.'
'I don't like you' said the boy.
'Don't talk to me like that' said the doctor.
The boy said 'I'm going to get my toy.'

The boy went up to his room
He played with his bear.
It was brilliant
He pretended his bear was in its lair.

**Shona Bell  (7)**
**Calderwood Primary School**


# The Lazy Dog

There once was a dog
His name was Pal Tup
He ran away from home
In case his family gobbled him up.

He ran very fast and hid in a bin
And lay there very quiet
He lay there so long he had no food
He was on a very special diet.

He got out of the bin in search of some food
He sniffed at some bags but it was not too good.
So he went to the butcher's in search of some meat,
The butcher was kind so he gave him a treat.

**Morven Bell  (7)**
**Calderwood Primary School**

# The Big Fat Pig

Once there was a pig called Jo
He loved lying in bed, eating his bread.
He walked and walked and hurt his toe,
Because he was so fat he fell down below.

Then he popped up and rubbed his toe
To the chicken he said 'Hello.'
He didn't know the chicken.
Why he did that, I don't know!

**Pamela Blair  (7)**
**Calderwood Primary School**


# A Walk In The Park

I went for a walk in the park before it got dark.

I saw a cat it had black and white marks on its back.

It rushed away in a fright
'Cause it was late in the night.

I cycled home before it got really dark
I rushed away to get home safely.

**Carly Wilmott  (7)**
**Calderwood Primary School**


# The Bad Side Of Me

When I was a small boy
It was a bore
But then I took a peep in my dad's store
And I saw a big box of mayhem!
I looked I found a catty and a little toy ratty.
Some caps from my gun and I had some fun.

**Ronan Duff  (7)**
**Calderwood Primary School**

# Whenever I'm In Bed

Whenever I'm in bed
I certainly dream a lot
And think of lots of little
Monsters crawling
In my bed.

Whenever I'm in bed
I get a little sleep
And wake up in the
Afternoon as hungry
As a sheep.

Whenever I'm in bed
It gets really dark
I imagine all these
Ghosts and witches
Flying around my
Bed.

**Kieran McDonald  (9)**
**Carolside Primary School**

# What Shall I Draw

What shall I draw?
Draw a house
What shall I draw on the house?
Draw four white window panes.

What shall I draw in the garden?
Draw a path
But the path's leading out to the gate
Should I draw some flowers in a dirt patch
Is that it?

No, colour the gate red, the house and panes white
Loads of grass and the path has got to be peach.

**Jennifer Stuart**
**Carolside Primary School**

# My Dog

My dog is called Sooty
He's as black as soot
He has small bits of white in his toes
And a tiny bit down his chest.

My dog has brown eyes
Like my dad's
He is still young
He's only two and a half to be precise.

My dog can still jump my dog can still run
He is still very, very young!
He likes to guard and watch our house
He sometimes walks with not
Even a lead.

**Stuart McInnes  (9)**
**Carolside Primary School**


# My Weirdest Dream

My weirdest dream
was when I was God.
My magical power turned
me into a frog.

My saddest dream
was when I left my family.
I sailed away in a big boat
called Victoria.

My funniest dream
was when I went to the circus.
The clown told the jokes
and it made me laugh.

**Stephen Shindler  (9)**
**Carolside Primary School**

# My Dream Pet

For one quarter I'd have a dog
That barks at people I don't like
It would be playful and eat meat
And maybe cycle on a bike!

The next quarter would be a horse
Where I could always have a ride
It would eat hay and yellow oats
And could gallop across the River Clyde.

My second-last quarter would be a unicorn
That has a horn and flies
It would use its horn against people
And would know if I told lies.

The last quarter would be a deer
An animal that would prance
But also quite a shy animal
That couldn't prance to France!

So that was my dream animal
That I hope I could get
But if it does come out
I'll buy it and use it as my dream pet!

**Claire Hamilton  (10)**
**Carolside Primary School**


# Football

Running around the football field,
with the ball always clipping your heel.
After half-time your bottle is sealed,
and after the game they have a meal.

The next game was just the same,
and they got beat and the keeper was to blame.
The manager was so angry they got beat
And all he had for dinner was a big bit of meat.

**Stuart Taylor  (10)**
**Carolside Primary School**

# One Day In The Middle Of The Night

I woke from sleep in the middle of the night
In the garden there was a huge animal totally white.

When I stared at it from my window
It gave me a fright.
It had only one eye and two wings
That could fly
A red pointy nose and a big white head.
So I dived under the covers and back to bed.

When I woke in the morning
I looked out again
To look for the animal that had caused me pain
I remembered the snow from the day before.

Gosh, Frosty the snowman was no more.

**Kathryn Wylie (9)**
**Carolside Primary School**


# Cara My Cousin

Cara my cousin is very funny
She is very sunny
She likes to play
And laugh all day
Her little blue eyes
Are lit up with joy
She likes to play with her princess toy.

She is very happy
She doesn't wear a nappy
She likes to sing as she swims
She likes to watch the Fimbles
She likes to drink Fruit Shoots
Although she is very cute!

That's my little cousin!

**Lindsay Robertson (10)**
**Carolside Primary School**

# There's A Monster!

There's a monster in my house
Who lives under my bed.
Is it the figure I imagine in my head?
Is he blue or is he red?
*He is alive and not dead!*

He might reach out and grab me!
When I'm fast asleep.
What if he has a gun?
For one thing he's not fun.
He kicks my bed, taps me on the head
I try to forget the things he said.

Should I go down and take a peek?
Should I feed him carrot or leek?
It's worth a try or maybe not,
Will I feed him an awful lot?
After that he might be kind to me
*I'll do it! 1, 2, 3!*

**Grant Cairney (9)**
**Carolside Primary School**


# John The Porky Penguin

I know a porky penguin
Who set up a deckchair on the lawn
He eats chocolate and lots of sweets
He eats anything that kids call treats!

Blimey! He would eat the cat
If it had a layer of chocolate or something like that.
He would eat the world and the Milky Way
But one small problem, he is here to stay!

**Callum Carmichael (10)**
**Carolside Primary School**

# Sleepovers

Sleepovers are fun,
When they have begun.
It feels like we're free,
So we watch lots of TV.
I share sweets and candy,
With my friend Mandy.
My mum gets mad,
When she sees what we've had.
My mum slams the door,
When we ask to eat more.
We all get a fright,
When I turn off the light.
I quietly peep
To see if the others are asleep.
So this is what my sleepovers are like.

**Sarah Wilson (9)**
**Carolside Primary School**


# My Dreams

I don't know what I dream about
Something that's loud and small
I don't know what I dream about
I don't know at all.

It tries to bite me on the leg
It is really, really sore
It tries to bite me on the leg
Oh stop it! No more.

I don't know what I dream about
Something with a fat belly.
I don't know what I dream about
Oh, it's my sister Kelly.

**Laura Briggs (9)**
**Carolside Primary School**

# I'm A Celebrity, Get Me Out Of Here!

J  is for John who walked out halfway through
U  is for underground where Jennie had to go
N  is for naughty, trust me that's what Peter is
G  is for guinea-pig, that's what Diane is
L  is for Lord Brocket, his real name's Charlie
E  is for end, I've finally come to it.

**Alexander Hannah  (9)**
**Carolside Primary School**


# Teachers

T  is for teachers annoying and boring
E  is for everything that is quite a big pain in the school
A  is for art with paint-flinging brushes
C  is for chewing gum stuck on the walls
H  is for home which I can't wait to be in
E  is for everyone trying to have some pleasure with their friends
R  is for raging teachers which get angry quite easily
S  is for some people who tell on you every day.

**Jacob Hong  (9)**
**Carolside Primary School**


# Snowman

S  now is falling on the ground
N  o human footsteps can be seen
O  nly tracks of cats and foxes
W  ind their way around the houses
M  any children wake up
A  nd dash outside to have some fun
N  ow the snow is falling fast.

**Fraser McDougall  (9)**
**Carolside Primary School**

# Sport

Sport is a challenge
to us all
old and young
small and tall

From football to swimming
from running to climbing
our health and fitness
will stop declining.

Sport gives us heroes
who we admire
their skills are something
to which we aspire.

Our heroes are great
our heroes are awesome
they entertain us through
winter, spring, summer and autumn.

**Jamie Meldrum (9)**
**Carolside Primary School**


# Lindsay

Lindsay is nice
Her nickname is Spice
She is very funny
When she smiles it gets sunny
When she cries it rains
But I cheer her up again
And then she doesn't cry.

Lindsay is pretty
She is kind but witty
She is my good friend
This is where the poem ends.

**Misha Palmer (9)**
**Carolside Primary School**

# My Best Friend

My best friend is Catriona
She's playful, funny, laughy and giggly
That's Catriona alright
Her ginger hair, her freckles too
Her Bear Factory animals, Honey, Tigger
Ringo and Sue
She likes Honey the best and I do too
Honey is a bear with a best friend Poppy
Whose ears are very floppy.

Catriona loves choccie biscuits
Playmobile too
She loves to eat and beat her sister
and brother
She's the best friend I've ever had
and hope I'm hers too.

**Ailish Ross  (9)**
**Carolside Primary School**


# The Differences In Animals!

Lions and tigers make a *loud* noise
unlike a little tortoise.

Gorillas are black and have a strange back
But they climb trees slower than monkeys.

Rabbits like to jump up and down
I think they could bounce downtown.

Birds are fast and live in trees but
luckily they don't get fleas.

Bees like honey and don't have any money
They go mad if someone is bad.

**Laura McIntyre  (10)**
**Carolside Primary School**

# I Know A Monster!

I know a monster
That lives under the bed
I know a monster
And its name is Ted

He likes to growl
He likes to bark
He likes to run
And chase a shark

But one day
He ran away
And I never saw him again
But I know he's out there
As happy as can be.

**Andrew Cuthbert  (9)**
**Carolside Primary School**


# My Best Friend

My best friend is tall and blond
And funny all the way through
My best friend is a lovely chap
And never stops smiling.

My best friend is pretty smart
And takes on any challenge
My best friend can be serious
But normally he's not.

My best friend has a Border collie
That's small and black and cute
My best friend is nice and cheery
And my best friend is Scott.

**Douglas Young  (9)**
**Carolside Primary School**

# The Monster Under The Bed

I can hear the moans and groans coming from under
the bed
I can see the shadow the size of a pillow.

I can smell the smell of a pig that fell in the sewer.

I wonder why the monster is under my bed?
I wonder what he's doing under my bed?
I wonder when he got there?
I wonder when he's going to leave?

I can't stand the sounds for I can't get to sleep
I can't stand the sight of the shadow for it freaks me
out
I can't stand the smell because it rots my nose

*I wish he would leave!*

**Craig Imrie  (10)**
**Carolside Primary School**


# Sleepover

I'm having a sleepover at my house,
But unfortunately we have a mouse.
We're going shopping before the party
And getting goodies to make it hearty.

Now it's time to have some fun,
But someone's on the run
When we got her back,
She was wearing a sack.

We told stories about scary beasts
And had our midnight feasts
In the morning we got up early
Then they went away merrily.

**Catriona McCallum  (9)**
**Carolside Primary School**

# War

Tony Blair, Tony Blair
George Bush, George Bush
They are crazy men
Going to war for no reason
I don't think they ever thought it through.

Many men died, many men died
Women and children killed
Bang! Bang! They must have thought
But the man that brought terror to his country
Is banged up in jail.

Nuclear bombs, nuclear bombs
We found none so why war?

Iraqi people can live in peace thanks to the brave men
I am so relieved that the world is safe again
Thanks to the brave men that risked their lives.

This poem is for the men and women that died saving us
from destruction.

**Calum Husenne  (10)**
**Carolside Primary School**


# My Funny Family

My dad has a very short memory
When he wants milk he goes to the chemistry
My mum is shopping mad
If she doesn't go she gets quite sad
My brother is football crazy
He sits and watches football, he's very lazy
My sister loves Winnie the Pooh
She likes Tigger, Eeyore and even Roo
Me, well I'm quite ordinary
But my family is quite extraordinary.

**Robyn Adams  (9)**
**Carolside Primary School**

# Jumping On My Bed

Sometimes I jump upon my bed,
And think, *oh no I'll bump my head.*
But now I know it's just alright,
I nearly gave myself a fright.

Sometimes I jump upon my bed,
And fall back and hurt my head.
But now I know it's just a bump,
I think I've got a big, big lump.

Sometimes I jump upon my bed,
And think that I will break my head.
But now I know not to scream,
Because it was a really good dream.

**David MacDonald (9)**
**Carolside Primary School**


# Space

Moonlight, sunlight and clouds
All in space, why oh why
Does space go so high?

Moonlight, sunlight and clouds
Clouds are so soft and big
Sunlight is so bright.

Moonlight, sunlight and clouds
The sun is so hot, the moon is so bright
I don't know why but it is all a
beautiful sight.

**Emma Robertson (9)**
**Carolside Primary School**

# My Family Poem

My dad cooks the dinner in our house
He's loads of fun
And plays with me in the sun.
He's the best!

My mum washes the dishes
And sometimes feeds the fishes
And in the mornings she needs a rest.
She's the best!

And as for me
I help them out
But most of the time I am allowed to
Play about.
And altogether our family is the best!

**Holly Dryden (9)**
**Carolside Primary School**


# Our Crazy Headteacher

We have a crazy headteacher
He's really raving mad
But he doesn't do a thing
If anyone is bad.

He's never really serious
And he barely gets things done
So we've had complaints
From many, many mums.

Even in the playground
He's always causing trouble
He does many strange things
Honestly, they're weird and
wonderful.

**Molly Corcoran (9)**
**Carolside Primary School**

# The Hills

These are the great hills,
With no paths, trees or mills.
I climb them most of the time,
And have an orange, apple and lime.

When I reach the top of the hill,
I feel sick, so I take a pill.
I look down and see for a view,
A lovely lake the colour of blue.

By the time I reach the top gate,
I'm going to be home very late at eight.
When I get home I'm not seen,
But no! Mother comes in and says,
'Where have you been!'

**Sara Kettlewell (9)**
**Carolside Primary School**


# My Crazy Teacher

I have a crazy teacher
Who is called Mrs Bleacher
She's really funny
And walks like a bunny
But the only thing is her mobile always rings
And she always forgets to turn it off and says, 'Oh jings.'

She's the best teacher I've ever had
Once she said to one of the boys 'You're a good lad'
I remember once she made Alex laugh so much he began to burst
Then after that, our crazy teacher was cursed.

**Emma Appleyard (9)**
**Carolside Primary School**

# Autumn

Summer has gone, autumn is here
Different sights to see
Bare trees
Juicy fruit ready to eat
Summer has gone
Autumn is here
Animals collecting nuts
for hibernation
Leaves make a royal carpet
As they flutter gently to the ground
The grumbling combine going by
Makes the squirrels scamper by
Autumn has come in a wink
of an eye
Time to get ready for bed.

**Nichola Pinkerton  (10)**
**Chapelgreen Primary School**


# My Autumn Poem

Summer has gone, autumn is here
Days get shorter, fingers tingle
Trees show off their golden coats
Leaves twist and spin
As they flutter to the shiny ground
The leaves fall down like ballerinas
Twirl and twist all day long
Let the night shine and let the ripe juicy
Brambles taste good
This is the start of autumn.

**Angela Dunbar  (10)**
**Chapelgreen Primary School**

# My Autumn Poem

Autumn has come
Leaves are falling like swirling dancers
Making a beautiful carpet
Ripe, juicy brambles ready to pick
Sparkling dew on the grass in the morning
Autumn is great.

**Graeme Marklow  (11)**
**Chapelgreen Primary School**

# The Spot

I walked in the bathroom and turned on the light.
I looked in the mirror; saw a hideous sight.
I screamed at the thing on my face,
It was worse than toilet paper trailing from lace.
Mum came running on the dot,
'What is it, what is it? Awww my baby's first spot.'
'How can you say that about this thing,
I wish it could go in just one ping.'

'Wash your face, it might just be a mark,
Next time don't scream, you sound like a dog's bark.
Now come a little closer, let's get a peek,
Wash again, there's tomato sauce from last week.'
'Argh and there's the spot,'
'What are you screaming at, it's just a wee dot.'
'Am I hearing right? Just a wee dot,
How can you say that? You can see it a lot.'

'Oh no school pictures tomorrow, what am I going to do?
I'm going to have to run and hide in the loo.'
'Oh! It's not bad you're just paranoid,
It's not like people will run and try to avoid.'
'Mum please can I take a day off, oh please?
If you don't let me, I'll shout and scream on my knees.'
'Oh my goodness, hee, hee, hee!
It's just a crumb, are you blind, can you see?'

**Shannon Lawson  (10)**
**Craighead Primary School**

# My Stocking

My stocking
is hanging
near the fireplace.
The colour is satin blue.
It's waiting to be filled
up to the brim
leaving not a space.
I move it on Christmas Eve
to the bottom of my bed,
sitting beside my favourite ted.
It's morning, I look inside
to see what might be there.
It's full of things like chocolate coins
and lots of things to eat.
My sister's in the room next door,
I say to her,
'Look inside!'

**Lorna Reid  (10)**
**Craighead Primary School**


# Is The Rainbow Tired?

Is the rainbow tired?
He's not come out all day
Why isn't the rainbow there?
Why won't he come to play?

Is the rainbow tired?
Why won't his colours shine?
Is the rainbow angry?
I hope he's feeling fine.

Is the rainbow tired?
Is he tucked up in his bed?
Goodnight Mr Rainbow
Go and rest your head.

**Lisa Main  (10)**
**Craighead Primary School**

# The Miserable Lion

I am a lion, big but not glad
Everyone makes fun of me and it makes me
Feel sad
They all make fun of me because I don't have
A mane, but those that do that are a really
Big pain
They didn't let me have lunch, I know it's not fair.
All I could find was a really juicy pear.
My tummy is rumbling I need something quick,
Oh there's a zebra I best go have a picnic.
They finally let me into the game
And they found the guy that was being a pain.
Oh, I have started to grow a mane!

**Andrew Quirk (9)**
**Craighead Primary School**


# Oh Brother

I have a younger brother who likes to play with dolls,
He may be crazy and stupid but he's not that bad at all,
Oh crazy little brother where have you gone now?
I know you've hidden somewhere so you don't need to frown,
My brother makes me laugh; my brother makes me cry,
I think he wants to punch me, see he will have to try and try,
But I really love my brother and I think he loves me too,
So if we're going to love forever then we must be true.

**Suzanne Nicholson (10)**
**Craighead Primary School**

# Where Is He?

Where is he, Mam?
Where is he?
I've looked all over the place, Mam,
I just don't see.

Has he gone away, Mam?
When's he comin' back?
I've checked all his favourite places, Mam
He might've been attacked!

Just tell me the truth, Mam,
Where's he gone?
I need to know what's happened, Mam,
This just isn't on!

Why is his bed empty, Mam,
And the sheets rumpled and creased?
Where's his mobile phone, Mam?
There's half his things gone, at least.

Where's his football top, Mam,
And his big red bag?
What about his rock star posters, Mam,
Or his rugby-team tag?

Why isn't he riding his bike, Mam,
Or climbing the big, old tree?
Why isn't he kicking his football, Mam?
Tell me, tell me, tell me!

What happened to his gold chain, Mam,
And his holey old jeans?
Where are his shabby blue trainers, Mam?

I just don't know what all this means.

**Laura Dover (9)**
**Craighead Primary School**

# On Motorcycles

On motorcycles up the road they came
In the distance
Bigger and bigger
My heart racing
My mind pondering
Where are they going?
Who are they?
Coming closer
Roaring louder
Covered from head to toe in leather
Engines purring
As they glided past
Where were they going?
Who were they?

**Calum Ronaldson  (11)**
**David Livingstone Memorial Primary School**


# If I Were In A Barn Owl's Ear

If I were in a barn owl's ear
I could hear . . .
A shooting star zoom through the sky,
The trees swaying in the wind,
The children getting taught at school and
People crying in Africa.
I could also hear . .
A popstar singing at a concert,
A fish swimming in the ocean,
Children playing on a beach and
An eskimo walking in the freezing cold.

**Carly McPhee  (11)**
**David Livingstone Memorial Primary School**

# Fear Is . . .

Fear is a dark hole that can go on forever,
Fear is a high cliff that you are edging off,
Fear is a wild jungle that you are walking through,
Fear is a deep, dark ocean, in which you have to
swim,
Fear is a dark, scary street with no one on it,
Fear is a dark thunderstorm going on over your head,
Fear is a massive, dark shadow leaning over you,
Fear is walking down a dark street at night with
teenagers drinking,
Fear is walking down an alley at night where homeless
people lie,
Fear is . . .

**Kirsten Darling (11)**
**David Livingstone Memorial Primary School**


# My Barn Owl's Ear

If I was in a barn owl's ear,
I could hear Mercury zooming past,
I could hear people talk in the distant
land,
I could hear the aliens in their UFO on
Mars,
I could hear the winner of the surf
contest in Australia,
I could hear my mum talking at work,
And most of all I could hear voices on
Pluto.

**Ross Burns (11)**
**David Livingstone Memorial Primary School**

# A Small Child's Rocking Horse

A small child's rocking horse,
Stored in the deepest corner of the attic,
Sitting behind old bags and boxes
In an imaginary land
For many years forgotten
Asking when it shall be found, if ever
Its wood and its eyes very dull
Its mouth closed tight
All day and night
Its mane very tangled and ragged
Rocking when someone walks past
A day, a month, a year goes by
Still sitting in that lonely corner
Hearing voices and sounds
More boxes being dumped
How long shall it stay?
With no one noticing it was lying there sad.
Something like this could be precious to people
Unfortunately not this family
So still it lays
Forgotten forever, this poor rocking horse.

**Lauren Munro (11)**
**David Livingstone Memorial Primary School**


# If I Was In A Barn Owl's Ear . . .

I could hear a person screaming miles away,
I could hear the sunset setting upon the bay.
I could hear a lion's roar in Asia or Africa,
I could hear a circus with all the people's laughter.
I could hear the red planet, Mars, spinning,
I could hear the shining stars twinkling,
I could hear a mouse squeaking from a very far distance,
And a chemical burning with some strange substance.

**Pamela Heaney (11)**
**David Livingstone Memorial Primary School**

# Little Sister

I like my sister's clothes
She wears shorts, trousers, skirts, dresses,
bobbles and clasps.
She is beautiful.

I like the places she goes and things she does.
She does kite flying
and she goes out in the garden or park
and plays on the swing or the chute.

I like the things she plays with
she has K-nex, Barbies,
a computer, Connect 4 and Lego.

She has all the things I'm too big for.
But most of all in the house
as long as we are together,
she shares her toys with me.
I love my sister.

**Monique Bennett  (10)**
**David Livingstone Memorial Primary School**

# Exhaustion Is . . .

Exhaustion is playing extra time in a
difficult football match.
Exhaustion is coming in from a
boring day at work.
Exhaustion is driving hugely
long distances.
Exhaustion is travelling to the
moon on a space rocket.
Exhaustion is fighting a war
that's lasted for years.

**David Kelly  (11)**
**David Livingstone Memorial Primary School**

# My Real Best Friend

My real best friend is not
Courtney,
        Rachel or Louise.
My real best friend
        used to live in my house.
He was barking mad about stuff.
He was always waiting in the hall
    for me to come back
            from school or my friend's.
He was very playful at times.
If someone came into my house
    he would run up to them
            like lightning.
I don't see him anymore
    because he is dead.

For my real best friend is my puppy Zack.

**Lauren Buddy (10)**
**David Livingstone Memorial Primary School**


# Bonfire Night

Everyone gathers in the park to watch the fireworks fly,
They hear the bangs whilst munching on marshmallows
And watching Guy Fawkes burn!

The people spin sparklers around and around
The weather is damp and cold
The children are all dressed up for the occasion
They are all cosy and warm.

Bonfire Night is over now.

But it will *return!*

**Lauren McKenzie (11)**
**David Livingstone Memorial Primary School**

# Magic Land

As I lay in my bed, drifting off to sleep
I could hear nothing, not even the slightest peep.
I cuddled into Mr Bear, his real name was called Ted
He was the king of all the teddies, that sat upon my bed.
I snuggled up close beside Mr Bear
His fur soft like a Cadbury cream.
Together we had drifted into a magical dream
All around us there were fairies, I couldn't believe my eyes.
Their wings fluttered around, oh what a surprise.
I skipped and ran and laughed with glee.
I was so happy, just bear and me.
I tossed and turned and much to my despair
I was back n my room, with no fairies there.

**Erin Dean  (12)**
**David Livingstone Memorial Primary School**


# Loneliness Is . . .

Loneliness is a homeless person on the streets
A dark room the size of the suitcase
A red turning brown and dying with no sunshine or water
An old park with nothing left but a swing that has
rusty chains
A book with no pictures not even any words
A farm with lawns needing to be cut with dirty
wool from a sheep,
A lonely star in the sky wishing for it to be a family
member,
A sad child with nothing to eat but small crumbs from
hard bread,
A dream where anything you need will not be seen.

**Clare Carruthers  (11)**
**David Livingstone Memorial Primary School**

# Seasons

Spring is in the air!
Spring is in the air!
Gardens lovely everywhere
Flowers blooming
Sunny days are here!

Summer is here!
Summer is here!
Picnics in the park
School breaks up
Extra hour out to play.

Autumn is here!
Autumn is in the air!
Leaves are falling from the trees
Windy days are here.

Winter is here!
Winter is here!
Wrap up warm
In the house
Out of harm.

Everybody is happy!

**Natasha Monteith (10)**
**David Livingstone Memorial Primary School**


# Owl Poem

If I were in a barn owl's ear I could hear . . .
Mars zooming past
And a little fish swimming in the sea.
I could hear a human's heart beating
And thunder striking 100 miles away.
I could hear the tide coming in and out
And a little ant moving around.

**Robert Gracie (11)**
**David Livingstone Memorial Primary School**

# Running Away!

That's it I'm running away
Or should I stay?
Nope
I've decided
I'm running away
What would Mum say?

I'm just running away!
Why did she have to shout?
What is this about?

I did nothing wrong.
That gives me more reason to run away.
Mum will tell me to stay,
But I'm not going to listen
I'm running away!

Hey!
OK!
I'll stay!

**Courtney Lanaghan  (10)**
**David Livingstone Memorial Primary School**


# Loneliness Is . . .

A bottomless pit with no echo to be heard
A soundless emotion in the middle of nowhere
A clock with no time to tell or say
A world with nothing but empty space
The last petal from the last red rose
A tear from someone with nowhere to go
A book with no pages or words to be read
A mirror with no reflections to be seen
A star with no twinkle in the night
A room with nothing but darkness all around
A shadow in which nothing is found.

**Sarah Brozio  (10)**
**David Livingstone Memorial Primary School**

# Going To School

In the morning I get up,
Have a drink, gulp, gulp, gulp,
Go back to bed and can't get up,
Wake up again!
Oh no! It's nine o'clock,
Rush to the loo, try to get out,
Lock's stuck!
Eventually get out, have breakfast, hurry up,
Get dressed, go to school,
It was a horrible, horrible day.

**Alysha Sommerville (10)**
**David Livingstone Memorial Primary School**


# Winter Poem

W hen it's cold all you want to do is curl up and go to sleep
 I nside it's warm and outside it's freezing
N obody but kids out
T rees are bare with a blanket of snow
E veryone is in bed early
R ain, snow, sleet and snowballs! When will it end?

**Emma Chambers (10)**
**David Livingstone Memorial Primary School**


# Winter

Winter is cold and snow means no school for everyone
I have to say it is bad to be cold
The howling wind at night usually gives me a fright
Enjoying playing in the snow with your pals
Rolling in the snow wishing that the day will never end.

**Graeme Goodall (10)**
**David Livingstone Memorial Primary School**

# Hunter, It's Really Not Fair

Hunter, leave it alone
Don't stand laughing
While it runs for its life
It fears you hunter.

Please leave it alone
Put yourself in its shoes
And see how frightened
It really is.

It's really not fair hunter
You're doing it for fun
It's terrified of you
And your gun.
So please
Leave it alone
It's really not fair
Hunter.

**Rachel McKinnon (10)**
**David Livingstone Memorial Primary School**


# I Love Snow

*Cold*
It is cold
And I have a scarf on
Hat, gloves and scarf on.

*Snowing*
Snow is falling
The car has been snowed in.
Children are happy sledging
Running mad everywhere.

*Quiet*
The motorway is very quiet
But our street is very noisy
Because we're outside playing!

**James MacGregor (10)**
**David Livingstone Memorial Primary School**

# Blizzard

I'm walking in a blizzard
I don't know where I am going
Snowballing would be fun
But I don't stop to pick any snow up
I'm getting colder and colder.

I'm in my house now
Nice and warm
The fire's on and I am drying off
The blizzard starts to die down.

Everywhere it's covered in a blanket of white
Now *I'll* have a snowball fight with my dad.

**Steven Clark  (10)**
**David Livingstone Memorial Primary School**


# The Fighter Jet

Hear it roar!
Hear it thunder!
Hear it crash!
Hear it trunder!

Watch as the propeller spins for lift-off,
Watch as the jet tilts to turn a corner.

Look at the rockets on each side,
Look at the guns on the wings.

Hear the engine roar through the sky,
Hear the fighter jet fly!

**Andrew Murphy  (10)**
**David Livingstone Memorial Primary School**

# Skateboarding

I like skateboarding.
It's fun
And I go fast.
Sometimes I crash.

I got my skateboard
For my birthday
And I fell!
But I still like skateboarding.

I like the wind in my face.
I like going fast.
It's thrilling!
It's exciting!

**Stuart Robertson  (10)**
**David Livingstone Memorial Primary School**


# Thank You Snow

*Thank you snow*
Thanks for the snowstorm.
Thanks for the snowmen.
Thanks for the snowballs.
Thanks for the snow angels.
Thanks for the sledging.
Thanks for the white streets and gardens
But most importantly

*Thanks for shutting school!*

**Fraser Jamieson  (10)**
**David Livingstone Memorial Primary School**

# A Pet

I have a pet
Who does not go to the vet
He hardly eats and always sleeps
He has long ears and a pink nose
He barks in the dark
So I get up and give him his toys
To keep him quiet for an hour or two
I feed him in the morning
And that's him for the rest of the day
When he eats he takes his time
I love my pet
I just wish he would eat more
He is as skinny as you could imagine.

**Laura Neillis (8)**
**David Livingstone Memorial Primary School**


# Snowfall

No break of wind
No beam of sun,
Hardly a whisper in the air,
Snowflakes falling like a gentle waterfall,
Children playing in the snowfall.

The only sound you can hear
Is the cries of delight
From the children.

A blanket of snow
A blanket of quiet
Covers the earth.

**Scott Henderson (10)**
**David Livingstone Memorial Primary School**

# Bullying

Bullies wait until you're alone.
Bullies demand things from you.
If you say no
They hit you or do anything to hurt you.
Then once they've got what they want.
They turn and walk away.
Then the next time they see you they
Threaten, torment and boast.
Your friends don't know how you feel inside
They don't know anything.
You can barely talk without getting
Angry.
You can barely eat
      Concentrate
      Or sleep.
You feel so hollow inside.
In the morning you know you have to go to
School so you get a shiver down your spine.
Will they hit you ten times harder?
They loom over you.
They have commanding eyes.
They follow you without you knowing
So you have to be careful.
Bullies make you lie.
Bullies make you do things you don't want to do.
Bullies are *horrible!*
Bullies put on an act of being tough.
*Bullies should change!*

**Leeanne Kennedy  (10)**
**David Livingstone Memorial Primary School**

# Storm

In my bed
I can hear the wind
Whistling past my window
I can hear thunder
I can see lightning
It was so scary
I jumped under my bed
Next I creep out from
My hiding place
And look out of the window.

Awesome!

**Alasdair Adams (10)**
David Livingstone Memorial Primary School

# Blizzard

B is for building snowmen
L is for laughing and having fun
I is for icy weather
Z is for the poor animals in zoos being cold
Z is for you can't see the zebra's white stripes
A is for ants struggling in the snow
R is for reindeer having fun
D is for playing with your dad and mum.

**Chloe Coventry (10)**
David Livingstone Memorial Primary School

# My Dog Sleeps Like A Log

My dog is brown and white
My dog is tiny
My dog is nice and cuddly
I love my dog.

**Bradley Inglis (7)**
David Livingstone Memorial Primary School

# Old Cellar

There is an old cellar down the road.
Whoever enters it would have to be bold.

I wouldn't go down there, nobody dares!
But then again, nobody cares.

I don't know what's down there, spider webs, ghosts.
Whatever is down there, I would hate the most.

Maybe who's there is homeless or lost.
But if it's a gang's lair I'll pay the cost.

**Derek Whiteford (10)**
**David Livingstone Memorial Primary School**


# My Dog

My dog rolls over
He runs away from me
I play with him when I am with my friends
He licks me on the cheek when I am working
He is black and brown with big paws
I take him for a walk each day
He is really funny
That's my dog.

**Taylor Farrell (7)**
**David Livingstone Memorial Primary School**


# My Skateboard

My skateboard is yellow
I got it when I was three
The wheels are red
I am good at skateboard handstands
I don't need protection
Even though sometimes I fall off.

**Daryn Smith (7)**
**David Livingstone Memorial Primary School**

# Thunder And Lightning

*Crack!* goes the thunder
*Flash!* goes the lightning
*'Help!'* said I.
As I ran for the bed.
I dived under the quilt.
And pondered what would it be like to be out in that storm.
I imagined the sounds there would be.

*Crack!*
*Argh!*
*Sizzle!*

**Christopher Irvine (10)**
**David Livingstone Memorial Primary School**


# My Cat

My cat is Felix
He is orange and white
He likes to eat mice
He is very nice
Though he scratches for food
He never eats it
And that's why I like him
My cat Felix.

**Scott McCormick (7)**
**David Livingstone Memorial Primary School**


# Brown Is For

Brown is for Crash Bandicoot saving Coco
Brown is for a rat scurrying fast
Brown is for a car zooming past
Brown is for brick for building a wall
Brown is for coins for buying things.

**Keir Johnson (7)**
**David Livingstone Memorial Primary School**

# My Hamster

My hamster is orange
So I called him Toffee
He bites people he doesn't know
He is cuddly and cute
I was so pleased when I got him
I don't know why he bites
He is only seven weeks old
I took him out last night
He is a great wee hamster to me
All the time.

**Andrea Dobbins  (7)**
**David Livingstone Memorial Primary School**


# A Star

When I am older
I will be a star
I will go to Hollywood
And play the guitar
I will practise my songs
And sing them out loud
Then I'll do some concerts
And my mum will be proud.

**Aimee Kane  (8)**
**David Livingstone Memorial Primary School**


# My Puppy

My puppy is called Ben
He is a Jack Russell
He shuffles in his basket
He likes to eat sweeties
That is my puppy, Ben.

**Joseph Steel  (8)**
**David Livingstone Memorial Primary School**

# I Know A Dog

I know a dog called Bonnie
She is sometimes crazy
And can be lazy
She loves to eat
She sleeps under my auntie's bed
When she gets up from her nap
She always rolls and jumps
When I leave I wish I could stay
But then I come again another day.

**Jamie Balsillie  (8)**
**David Livingstone Memorial Primary School**


# What Is Green?

Green is grass
Green is an army tank
Green is green cars
Green is the frog
That swims in the pool
Green is for go
Green leaves on the tree
Green is a tall hill
Green is my chair
That I sit on at school.

**Cameron Dean  (7)**
**David Livingstone Memorial Primary School**


# My Dog

My dog is called Sandy
He is white and cuddly
He likes to play fetch with me
And he always jumps on me
I love my dog.

**Gary Hughes  (8)**
**David Livingstone Memorial Primary School**

# My Hamster

My hamster is called Harry
He nibbles at your fingers
He is black and white
He is cute
He is soft and cuddly
He plays in his ball
When I let Harry out
He hides under the couch
I love Harry.

**Abbey McInulty  (7)**
**David Livingstone Memorial Primary School**


# Blue

Blue is the sky
Where birds like to fly
A sea with splashing waves
Where dolphins swim
Blue is my jumper
I have to wear to school
Blue are my eyes
I use to read my book.

**Rachel Irvine  (8)**
**David Livingstone Memorial Primary School**


# Felix

My dog sleeps like a log
My dog is brown
And his eyes are blue
My dog likes chasing birds
And he runs away from me
He is called Felix
I love my dog.

**Jordan McTaggart  (7)**
**David Livingstone Memorial Primary School**

# Doggy

My dog is four
He uses his head
To slam the door
He spills his water
On his food
Then he won't eat it
Because it's not good
His name is Falco
He doesn't bother about cats
But he does like to sleep on mats.

**Rachel Darling  (8)**
**David Livingstone Memorial Primary School**


# My Cat

My cat is fat
My cat is lazy
My cat is one year old
My cat is black
My cat is noisy
Her eyes are brown
She sleeps like a log
Her name is Fushia
I love my cat.

**Rebecca Carruthers  (6)**
**David Livingstone Memorial Primary School**


# My Myna Bird

He's chatty
Always at night
He repeats what I say while he's flying
He speaks silly French.

**Andrew Hutcheson  (8)**
**David Livingstone Memorial Primary School**

# My Gran's Cat

He bites my fingers
He fights with Sammy
He catches mice
And leaves them in the hall
When I leave
He watches me from the
Window
Wondering when I will come back.

**Hollie Tavendale (7)**
**David Livingstone Memorial Primary School**


# My Dog

I got my dog
When I was seven
My dog is yellow
And he chases his tail
He runs about a lot.

**Jack Conner (7)**
**David Livingstone Memorial Primary School**


# When I Grow Up

When I grow up I want to win a cup
Hopefully I will, but I don't know if I will have the will
I might take bad pills but I might still win the ultimate cup.

When I grow up I might be a football player
And before I go on the pitch
I might do a prayer.

When I grow up I might play golf
I might be a dolphin
Or a big fat fish
But that is only a wish!

**Jordan Gallagher (11)**
**Glenmanor Primary School**

# When I Grow Up

When I grow up
I think I'll be
A lifeguard
That lives at sea.

I could be a swimmer
And swim all day
I will beat the swimmers
On the racing day.

I could be a boxer
And fight in the ring
I will fight Mike Tyson
And listen to crowds sing.

When I grow up
I think I'll be
An agent
With a golden key.

I could be a footballer
And I won't have to pay
I will do my keepyups
And play on Saturday.

Yeah that will be me.

**Craig Berry  (11)**
**Glenmanor Primary School**

# When I Grow Up

When I grow up
I think I'll be
A footballer
Living in fantasy.

I could be a tennis player
That practices all day
And when it comes to playing
I'll blow everyone away.

I could be a pilot
That flies up in the sky
And when I pass the children
I will wave bye-bye.

I could be a teacher
That would not say be quiet
Instead I'd say today for a change
Let's have a lovely riot.

I could be a soldier
That fights in the war
I could be the army leader
And a tank driver.

**Christopher McGovern  (11)**
**Glenmanor Primary School**

# When I Grow Up

When I grow up
I think I'll be,
A famous pop star
With plenty of money.

I could be like Barbie
And drive a big pink car
And put on my make-up
From a big round jar.

I think I'll be a lawyer
In a great big court,
And parade about so
Proudly with my curly wig.

I could be a post girl
And drive a big red bike
And drive all around town
To deliver letters to people that I like.

I could be a superhero
Called Super Dooper Girl
Except I would be beautiful
With my great pink pearls.

**Nicole Marsland  (10)**
**Glenmanor Primary School**

# School

Playtime is great
Playtime is fun
I love playtime, I hate when it's done
We play football, tig and sometimes even hide-and-seek
But we tidy up after we've played.

When it is done we trail into class
For our teacher to teach us about glass.
We write poems all day that don't even rhyme
But who cares I can get it to go with a chime.

When lunchtime is done
I am glad to go in
We have art on Monday
Our teachers are great,
And so is the school.
Well that is about it
And here is the end
I love this school.

**Natalie Dyer  (11)**
**Glenmanor Primary School**

# Scary Mary

Scary Mary quite contrary
How does your graveyard grow?
With monsters, cooks, assorted spooks
And headstones all in a row, row, row
Headstones all in a row.

**Jamie Horne  (11)**
**Hillhead Primary School**

# The Big Cream Bird

I was on my way to football
To go play with my team
I looked up and saw a bird
His feathers were cream.

It came flying down
Swooped me off my feet
I went flying up
When I started to feel the heat.

He took me to his volcano lair
All fiery and bright
I began to notice
All about the height.

He took me to all his friends
Those big and beautiful birds
Then suddenly we were away
Back home *hurray!*

**Gregg Boyd (10)**
**Hillhead Primary School**


# The Ring

It is the ring of Saturn.
It is a ball with a hole.
It is a face with no features.
It is a fried egg with no yolk.
It is a gold ice cream.
It is a sharpener with no hole.

**Kirsty Chalmers (11)**
**Hillhead Primary School**

# Summer's Here At Last!

It's summertime at last,
We're on holiday,
The birds, the trees, the plants and the sun
Have all come out to play.

Tomorrow we're off to Spain
To stay the week by a beautiful bay.
Soon we'll be dancing in the warm, golden sand,
Under the bright sunray.

Yippee, yippee, we're here at last,
In the sun and the fun, in the country of Spain.
On the beaches, in the oceans,
We will see the sun.
In the sand and the water,
We will have good fun.

Hip, hip, hooray,
The summer's been great fun,
But now it's back to work and school,
The term, has just begun!

**Sarah Airlie (10)**
**Our Lady of the Annunciation Primary School**


# Elephant

E xtra large and grey
L ikes to live in a herd
E ats lots of fruit
P lays in water and mud
H as a very long trunk
A lways remembers
N ever forgets
T ake care of each other.

**Daniel Squire (10)**
**Our Lady of the Annunciation Primary School**

# Music

Music is not just pop, rock and R 'n' B
There are many types for all to hear
Country, classical and folklore
To suit anyone's ear.

Often used are
Guitars, drums, bass and pianos
Don't forget
Flutes, trumpets, bagpipes and cellos.

Music is loved by all ages
Teenagers, adults, elders and the young.
Over the seas and in different places,
In different languages music is sung.

**Louise Gregory  (10)**
**Our Lady of the Annunciation Primary School**


# Seasons

Spring is the season
When baby lambs are born
Daffodils open out.

Summer is the season
When most people are at the beach
Lots of children playing at the park.

Autumn is the season
When the trees lose their leaves
Children kicking them everywhere.

Winter is the season
When children are out playing in the snow
Hats, scarves and gloves are worn.

**Catriona Jordan  (10)**
**Our Lady of the Annunciation Primary School**

# The Downfall Of The Dark Lord

L ost was a ring that has decided to show
O n the quest is the ring bearer Frodo,
R ingwraith's always in tow, and the
D ark Lord Sauron doesn't even know.

O sgiliath's about to fall, Sauron's army's marching
F aramir rides out, but cannot kill them all.

T he King of Gondor's coming, and behind
H im Legolas and Gimli are running
E ver to Minas Tirith, which is quite stunning.

R anks of Orcs flee from Gondor
I nto Mordor, where Frodo is struggling
N ear to the Cracks of Doom.
G ollum and the Ring fall in with a boom
S auron is defeated, peace is restored and the shadow of
evil will never again loom.

**Max Graham  (10)**
**Our Lady of the Annunciation Primary School**


# Lions

L ions are kings of the jungle and the kings of hunting
I n hunting they hunt in prides or hunt themselves and
kill young zebra and other kinds of animals
O n most days males fight with other males to become
leader of the pride or fight over lionesses
N ow lions have giant teeth that are as sharp as razors
S o never try to hurt lions because they will end up getting
you first.

**Matthew Paterson  (10)**
**Our Lady of the Annunciation Primary School**

# Spike The Alien

Spike the alien comes from Gardon
And has a red and purple horn
Spike the alien likes to play football
And Spike the alien is really quite tall.

Spike the alien has three small eyes,
And his tears are red when he cries
Spike the alien's feet have two toes
And Spike the alien has no nostrils in his nose.

Spike the alien has spikes all over his body
And his best friend's name is Jasco Crody
Spike the alien likes to have fun
And Spike the alien is number 1!

**Shannan Wilkie  (10)**
**Our Lady of the Annunciation Primary School**


# The Snake

I am the snake
I have an evil eye
And my venom
Could kill a lot of people.

I am the snake
I am a crushing, wicked, old snake,
I have a lot of poison.

I am the snake
I am enormous
I spit and hiss at my prey.

I am the snake
Long and slithering, old but fine
I have killed a lot in my time.

**Conor Clafferty  (10)**
**Our Lady of the Annunciation Primary School**

# Seasons

I like spring . . .
Shoots shoot from the ground to make new flowers in time
For summer
Days are longer, nights are shorter
I like spring do you?

I like summer . . .
The blazing sun making you sweet
The sun's heat making your clothes stick to you
Eating ice lollies on the roasting beach
I like summer do you?

I like autumn . . .
Leaves falling off the trees leaving them bare
Days are short and nights are long
Everybody preparing themselves for winter
I like autumn do you?

I like winter . . .
Days are short and nights are long
The trees topped with thick white snow
And seeing all the jaggy icicles hanging from the cars
I like winter do you?

**Aidan Russell  (10)**
**Our Lady of the Annunciation Primary School**

# Snake

S  nake rushing across the sand to catch its prey
N  asty venom running through its body
A  lways alert and ready to fight
K  icking into action when another snake attacks
E  ating its prey with delight after its heroic fight.

**Ross Hannah  (10)**
**Our Lady of the Annunciation Primary School**

# Return Of The King

R ejoice and be glad
E vil is destroyed
T errible deeds overcome
U nder the shadow of evil
R evealed is the light
N o war shall come to Middle-Earth again

O ver all great Hobbits,
F rodo, Sam, Merry and Pippin will lie as it was they who
   destroyed the evil of Mordor

T he King Aragorn is returned to the throne of Gondor
H elped did he in the struggle of war
E lessar his other name and rule he will for a great period

K illed is every Orc
I n Mordor no refuge could be found
N azgul destroyed, as was the Ring
G reat things were done and the end of Mordor.

**Michael Mullaney (10)**
**Our Lady of the Annunciation Primary School**


# Spider Poem

Spiders have eight legs
They crawl up things and down things
Some spiders are hairy, some are not
Some spiders are big and some are small
Some small spiders can jump
Some spiders stay very still
Some spiders stay in the same place for a while.

**Roisin Gallacher (10)**
**Our Lady of the Annunciation Primary School**

# Seasons Of The Year

In spring flowers start to grow tall
While birds call as if they are trying to talk to me.

In summer the sun is shining for everyone to see
As they play with their friends happily.

In autumn children stamp on the crunchy leaves
That have fallen from the bare-looking trees.

In winter people sledge down the hill full of snow
Screaming as it starts to go
Snowflakes fall all around
And quickly melt on the dirty, cold ground.

**Kathryn Murphy (10)**
**Our Lady of the Annunciation Primary School**


# All About Cats

Cats need to be fed
Cats need to drink water
Cats need to be able to play
Cats need lots of attention
Cats need to be healthy.

Cats like to drink milk
Cats like to play with wool
Cats like to get treats
Cats like to go to sleep
Cats like to run about.

**Angela Traynor (10)**
**Our Lady of the Annunciation Primary School**

# Winter Gardens

Under an old house far, far down
lived a hairy mole
He was waiting for someone to pop out
and say hello.

Through the long overgrown grass
a snake slithered through the wild field
spying a rat screaming by.

Tucked in a small ball
a prickly hedgehog
popped out to see the world.

On a large green leaf
a red and black ladybird
dreamed about her children.

**Louise Reilly & Lewis Howie  (9)**
**St Hilary's Primary School, East Kilbride**


# Winter Gardens

Under a medium stone lived a friendly frog which was overgrown
Looking for some water in a pond.

Underneath a tattered shed lived a suspicious spider
That was nearly dead.
Dreaming of people in his bed with his teddy Ted.

In the bushes and in the forest
Lived a stingy wasp.
Stinging people that went into his precious home.

In the blue sky flew a colourful bird
Catching wriggly worms for her hungry babies
And their proud dad.

**Callum Little  (8)**
**St Hilary's Primary School, East Kilbride**

# Tigger!

Tigger you're just the best,
Better than all the rest!
Your tail is super bouncy and long,
We all love it when you sing your bouncy song.

Winnie the Pooh, Tigger two, Piglet three, Eeyore four,
I know, I'll get a new teddy bear of you and put it right
Next to your door!

When you play hide-and-seek you're always the best at
Hiding!
But when it's snowing and the sun isn't glowing,
You are up on a big hill sliding.

Tigger lives in the Hundred Acre Wood,
With all his pals and friends,
But from this day on and in my heart,
This story will never end!

**Emma Anderson (11)**
**St Hilary's Primary School, East Kilbride**


# Winter Gardens

Beneath a damp stone
A thoughtful friendly frog
Is thinking about wet days to come.

Under the moist compost a wriggly worm moves quietly,
Waiting and waiting
For summer to come.

Under the muddy path,
A slimy snail
Is slithering around
Looking for its breakfast.

**Mark Edison & Alix Boylett (8)**
**St Hilary's Primary School, East Kilbride**

# School

At 9:00am the school bell rings
Ding-a-ling-ling-ding-ding-ding.
We work hard and start the day,
By hoping 3pm's not far away.
Maths and language, music too,
Colouring is red, green and blue.
Lunchbell rings, we chat about the day,
Running around - enjoying our play.
Return to class, go to PE
Lots of exercise - one, two, three!
Working on task, we count the seconds
Out to play home time beckons.
Three o'clock at last!
The day is past.
Escape the yard,
Go and play!
We're all so glad - it's Friday!

**Colette Baptie  (10)**
**St Hilary's Primary School, East Kilbride**

# Winter Gardens

Inside the massive trees
there are very stingy bees
looking for their next victim to come.

Under a big, heavy stone
lives a very pale snail
waiting for a mate to turn up.

In a cold, frozen pond
an extremely bouncy frog
awaits his next juicy snack.

**David McMonagle & Joshua Cairns  (8)**
**St Hilary's Primary School, East Kilbride**

# Winter Gardens

Outside a rusty old hut
A prickly hedgehog sat
Eating a juicy bug
Giving it a rare hard tug.

On a long high wall
An evil cat looks down low
Miaowing at the top of its voice
Miaow!

Up a gorgeous elm tree
A scampering squirrel
Is feeding on delicious chestnuts
And keeping them all to himself.

**Matthew Quinn (9)**
**St Hilary's Primary School, East Kilbride**

# Schools

School is such an annoying place
everyone thinks it's fun.
Everyone thinks you work at pace,
and they walk, never run.

'Can I maybe play your game?'
Stefano Di Vito says.
'No, it just won't be the same,'
And he runs to play with Des.

Now I am all alone
Walking here and there.
Someone then throws a stone,
And I swear!

**Stefano Di Vito (10)**
**St Hilary's Primary School, East Kilbride**

# Winnie The Pooh

Winnie the Pooh
Tigger, Piglet and Eeyore too.

Winnie the Pooh
Is a wee cuddly bear
And runs fast through the forest
Like a grizzly bear.

Tigger is a tiger
And jumps like a kangaroo
And when he is about
He always shouts *Boo!*

Piglet is a pink pig
And when she talks
She thinks she is big.

Eeyore is a lazy donkey
And sits around all day
But only really talks
When he has something to say.

These people are best friends
As all of you know
Their love for each other
Will never go.

**Simone Reilly (10)**
**St Hilary's Primary School, East Kilbride**

# Blue

Blue are the best band ever,
You know they're very clever,
They make up songs from the top of their head
I'm so glad they're not dead.

Blue are the best band ever,
The papers just don't know
They see them in their car and
Say they're moving to Hong Ko.

Blue are the best band ever
They never cry or shiver,
Even near a river

And that is why
Blue are the best band ever.

**Vicki Murdoch (11)**
**St Hilary's Primary School, East Kilbride**

# Monsters

Monsters are big, monsters are small
Monsters can be very tall
Monsters can be skinny, monsters can be fat
Monsters can just pop out of your hat
Monsters can be green, monsters can be blue
I wouldn't like to meet one, but would you?

Monsters are greedy they eat a lot of food
They would eat more than you ever could.
I'm sure they would try when you're walking by
They would have you for brunch, or better for lunch.

**Andrew Moran (10)**
**St Hilary's Primary School, East Kilbride**

# Piglet

Piglet is in Winnie the Pooh,
he gets a fright when someone says boo.
He is small and pink,
and goes to Owl when he needs to think.
He visits Eeyore in his old stick house,
the only thing is he is scared of a mouse.
He meets bouncy Tigger,
he asks him if he can get bigger.
He goes to Rabbit for a carrot,
but when he gets there, Rabbit is like a parrot.
He sees Winnie in the tree,
getting some honey for me.
The more and more cuddly toys I get
the more and more I'll never forget.

**Rachel Griffin (11)**
**St Hilary's Primary School, East Kilbride**


## Seasons

One day I woke up and found everything was covered in snow.
No flowers blooming.
All the lakes were frozen and all the animals were sleeping.
Just one colour; white all around.

One day I woke up and everything was growing.
The trees were budding and daffodils peeping.
Just one colour green.

One day I woke up and saw birds fluttering by.
The sun was shining and children playing.
Lots of colours all around.

One day I woke up and found everything was dying.
All the leaves were falling off the trees
And all the animals were collecting food about to go to sleep.
Just one colour, brown.

**Maria Smith (9)**
**St Machan's Primary School, Lennoxtown**

# The Battle Zone

They marched into battle
All armed and ready
But when they fought
They weren't so steady.
All they did was fight
For their lives
But in the end
They were taken with knives.
Blood and guts swept
Over the land
The hills, the moors, the earth and the sand.
People were lying
Injured and dead
Wishing they were home
Safe in their beds.
Some of them dead
Some barely alive
Those waiting at home
Asking why did they die?

**Andrew Allan (10)**
St Machan's Primary School, Lennoxtown


# Joy

Joy is green
It tastes like green and white Celtic chocolate
And smells like the green pitch at Parkhead.
So it must look like an honorary stadium.
Everyone thinks it sounds beautiful
Songs by the 60,000 fans.
A colourful rainbow shines across the pitch
It feels like paradise
Joy is like green and white stands.

**Christian McKenna (9)**
St Machan's Primary School, Lennoxtown

# Bears

Big bears
Small bears
Long bears
Short bears

Happy bears
Sad bears
Old bears
New bears

Black bears
Brown bears
Polar bears too

Whatever the shape or type they are
They're sure to scare
*You!*

**Josh Gallagher (10)**
**St Machan's Primary School, Lennoxtown**


# Dogs

Dogs sniffing at my feet
Dogs barking at the postman
Dogs growling at the door
Dogs just love to play!

Dogs sniffing round the trees
Dogs rolling in the muck
Dogs chewing cuddly toys
Dogs just love to play!

Dogs pawing at my door
Dogs snuggling on the bed
Dogs drifting off to Dreamland
Dogs just love to sleep!

**Melissa Ingleby (10)**
**St Machan's Primary School, Lennoxtown**

# My Brilliant Dog Brodie

Walking fast to school
Splashing in a puddle
Sniffing round a letterbox
My dog Brodie just likes to play!

Running in the park
Chasing after balls
Sniffing round a tree
My dog Brodie just likes to play!

Sitting at the telly
Licking at my hand
Sniffing at my clothes
My dog Brodie just likes to play!

Snuggled on my bed
Pawing at the sheets
Sniffing at my twitching toes
My dog Brodie just likes to sleep.

**Megan Pickett (10)**
**St Machan's Primary School, Lennoxtown**

# Ice Cream

Ice cream looks like the frothy waves
lapping over the shore.
Ice cream feels sticky as it melts in my hand.
Ice cream sounds like having fun on a warm
summer's day.
Ice cream smells like the best thing
on the planet,
Ice cream tastes like Heaven on Earth!

**Kerry Simpson (9)**
**St Machan's Primary School, Lennoxtown**

# My Gran

My gran is always kind to me
She listens to my troubles
She asks me if I've had a nice day
She gives me food and drink
She comes round for dinner
She childminds me.

She buys me lots of things
When she comes back from her holiday
She buys me clothes
She bakes me cakes and watches me play
She says I've got a great singing voice.

She lends me books to read
She's the coolest granny in the town
And I love her!

**Megan Duff  (9)**
**St Machan's Primary School, Lennoxtown**


# Pet Shop Rap

I've got a pet shop, a lively pet shop
A chirping, barking, squawking pet shop.
I've got a pet shop, a lively pet shop.
A splashing, dashing, scratching pet shop.

I've got tiny gerbils, prancing cats,
Cute little puppies,
Black and white rats.

I've got a pet shop, a lively pet shop,
A chirping, barking, squawking pet shop.
I've got a pet shop, a lively pet shop.
A spotted, striped multicoloured pet shop.

**Amy O'Donnell  (9)**
**St Machan's Primary School, Lennoxtown**

# Love

From me to you,
I'd like to say,
I love you more
And more each day.

I dream of you
From day to night,
Your hair so silky,
Eyes so bright.

Some people know
That I love you.
Some day I hope
You'll love me too.

**Fraser MacDonald  (9)**
**St Machan's Primary School, Lennoxtown**


# Ice Cream

Ice cream looks like snow
Ice cream feels freezing on my tongue
Ice cream sounds like an avalanche
It smells like Heaven
It tastes scrumptious.

**Dominic McMahon  (9)**
**St Machan's Primary School, Lennoxtown**


# Apples

Apples look like red snowballs
Apples feel crisp and smooth
Apples smell sweet
Apples sound crunchy in my mouth
Apples taste delicious.

**John MacDonald  (9)**
**St Machan's Primary School, Lennoxtown**

# Dylan

Dylan is playful
Dylan is fun,
She'll eat anything
Even a hot bun.

She's just like me
Though she lives in a hutch
People say she doesn't
Do that much.

She puts on special shows
And her little face glows.
I think she's great, I suppose

She's my Dylan!

**Hannah Sweeney (10)**
**St Machan's Primary School, Lennoxtown**


# School

School looks like prison
School feels hurtful
School sounds like a headache
School smells like a rotten fish
School tastes like a sore throat.

**Megan Griffin (9)**
**St Machan's Primary School, Lennoxtown**


# Ice Cream

Ice cream looks like snow
Ice cream feels soft
Ice cream sounds like magic
Ice cream smells like Heaven
Ice cream tastes like the best thing in the world.

**Thomas Rocks (9)**
**St Machan's Primary School, Lennoxtown**

# Anger

Anger is darkest black
It tastes like a dog's dinner
And smells like rotten chicken.
It looks like hell.
Anger sounds like thundering thunder
And feels like dragon's teeth.
Anger surrounds me.

**Ryan Wheeler  (9)**
**St Machan's Primary School, Lennoxtown**


# Spring

Spring is green
It tastes like honey made by busy bees
And looks like fields of swaying grass.
Spring smells like freshly cut flowers
And sounds like happy birds singing.
It feels like soft silk
Spring is all around me.

**Anna Turlewicz  (9)**
**St Machan's Primary School, Lennoxtown**


# Spring

Spring is sky-blue like a fresh new day,
It feels like newborn lambs, soft and cuddly,
And smells like freshly cut grass.
Spring tastes like sweet honey from busy bees.
It looks like red tulips swaying in the breeze,
And sounds like singing birds.
Spring is all around me.

**Claire McEntee  (9)**
**St Machan's Primary School, Lennoxtown**

# Love

Love is light red
it tastes like creamy soft caramel
and smells like a beautiful red rose.
Love sounds like romantic music
and looks like a nice box of chocolates
and feels emotional.
Love is everywhere.

**Michael Harkins  (9)**
St Machan's Primary School, Lennoxtown

# Love

Love is white
it tastes like Milky Ways
and smells like strawberries.
It looks like Heaven
and sounds like slow, emotional music.
Love feels like glittering snow.

Love is wonderful for you.

**Connor Hughes  (9)**
St Machan's Primary School, Lennoxtown

# Love

Love is red like a small, soft candle.
It tastes like a lovely smooth strawberry
And smells like a fragrant red rose.
Love looks like a big red heart.
It sounds like the birds in the morning.
Love is like nice soft silk.
    Love is soft!

**Eireanne Ovens  (9)**
St Machan's Primary School, Lennoxtown

# I Love My Precious Mum

My mum is a jolly bright yellow
She's crispy as a white winter,
And tastes like sweet caramel chocolate.
She's smooth sweet toffee.
Mum looks like a million big dollars.
She's smooth silky cotton
In a warm cosy living room.
Mum sounds like sweet birds singing.

   I love my mum to bits!

**Jordan McElhaney  (9)**
**St Machan's Primary School, Lennoxtown**


# Joy

Joy is yellow
It tastes like sweet juicy melons
And smells like clean fresh air.
It looks like stars twinkling brightly in the sky
And sounds like happy children laughing loudly.
It feels like a baby's soft skin.
   Joy is happiness!

**Gary McGhee  (9)**
**St Machan's Primary School, Lennoxtown**


# Ice Cream

Ice cream looks like snow
Ice cream feels soft
Ice cream sounds like ice sliding down a hill
Ice crem smells like Heaven
Ice cream tastes just perfect!

**Natalie Young  (9)**
**St Machan's Primary School, Lennoxtown**

# Love

Love is pink
It smells like a fragrant strawberry
And tastes like a juicy sweet apple.
Love looks like a stream of sweet happiness
And sounds like the purr of a cat out in the back alley.
Love feels like the fur of a bunny rabbit
Soft and warm.

      Love is all around.

**Elizabeth Carney  (9)**
**St Machan's Primary School, Lennoxtown**


# Love

Love is red
and smells like Marks and Sparks perfume
it sounds like a beautiful love song
and tastes like strawberry heart buttons.
Love looks like a romantic dove
it feels like a smooth, silky dress.
Love is great! Love is fun,
it always stays with me.

**Amy Magill  (9)**
**St Machan's Primary School, Lennoxtown**


# School

School looks like prison.
School feels like a nightmare.
School sounds noisy.
School smells like paint and glue.
School tastes like fish and chips.

**David Mackenzie  (9)**
**St Machan's Primary School, Lennoxtown**

# Love

Love is pink
It smells like a sweet scented candle
And tastes like smooth cremé caramel
It looks like the summer's sun; soft and warm.
Love sounds like the birds tweeting
It feels like smooth, soft silk.
Love is fun,
Love is romantic.

**Michelle Kearney (9)**
**St Machan's Primary School, Lennoxtown**

# Love

Love is pink
It tastes like smooth, dark chocolate hearts
And smells like strawberries.
It looks like the stars in the night sky
Love sounds like children playing in the sun
It feels like a soft cushion
Love is around me all the time.

**Kimberley McLarry (9)**
**St Machan's Primary School, Lennoxtown**

# If I Was . . .

If I was a footballer
I would be Thierry Henry
Oh, that's who I would be.

If I was a boxer
I would be Mike Tyson
Oh, that's who I would be.

If I was to choose who to be,
I would be,
        *Just me!*

**Darren McLean (9)**
**St Peter's Primary School, Partick**

# My Rat Is An Alien

My rat is an alien, his fur is bright furry white
I can't believe my rat is an alien.

My rat is an alien, he has the biggest, widest red eyes ever,
I can't believe my rat is an alien.

My rat is an alien, he has the longest pink tail ever,
I can't believe my rat is an alien.

My rat is an alien, he teaches on the planet Geranium,
I can't believe my rat is an alien.

My rat is an alien, he came to Earth for a holiday
I can't believe my rat is an alien.

My rat is an alien, but he's *my* alien.

**Megan McMenamin  (9)**
**St Peter's Primary School, Partick**

# If . . .

If my school was chocolate
it would be a Dairy Milk bar
warm and nice to eat.

If my goldfish was a fruit
it would be an orange, round and plump.

If my sister was a flower
she'd be a daisy, lovely to look at.

If the world was a ball,
it would be yellow, sunshine and happiness all around.

**Michelle McGurn (9)**
**St Peter's Primary School, Partick**


# The Beach

If my mum was a colour she'd be red
the colour of fury!

If my dad was a tree he'd be an oak tree
tall and strong!

If my sister was a sweet, she'd be a bit of chewing gum
that goes on and on and on!

**Ciaran McClymont (9)**
**St Peter's Primary School, Partick**

# The Crazy Place

When I went to a planet in space
it was so cool
it was great!
Then I went to the moon,
and got some cheese
and watched the shooting stars,
a shooting!
Finally I returned to Earth
and told my stories
            over
                  and
                        over
                              again!

**Amy Smart  (9)**
**St Peter's Primary School, Partick**


# If I Were . . .

If my mum were a biscuit
She would be a Jammy Dodger
Soft on the inside but hard on the outside.

If my brother were a colour
He would be green
Like his favourite team.

If my nana were a flower
She would be a rose
Nice but prickly.

Oh if only . . .

**Rachael McDonald  (9)**
**St Peter's Primary School, Partick**

# Good Times

As I went through the photos
Of many years ago
I came across some memories
Memories of, you know.

The laughing and the joking
Carrying on and having fun
The days, the hours of joy
I remember everyone.

The ones where I was little
And the embarrassing things I did
But everyone found it funny 'cause
I was just a little kid.

Then the ones where I was older
And loved to sing and dance
The countless moments I spent
Sat there in a trance.

The ones where I was older yet
I think I was in my teens
And I found some strange pictures that
I have not yet seen.

Lastly I found the ones from not so long ago
I realised I had changed as I sat there and looked
I wasn't that little kid anymore
And then I closed the book.

I placed it on the shelf again
For it was in the past
Then return to the family
I had got at last.

Even though the photo album
Is next to my cleaning chart
The memories in it
Will remain deep inside my heart.

**Katrina Crickett (11)**
**St Timothy's Primary School, Greenfield**

# Seasons

Watch out, watch out
Spring is about
There's chicks in the air
And flowers peeping out.

Watch out, watch out
Summer is about
People on the beach having ice cream
The sun beating down glistening on the stream.

Watch out, watch out
Autumn is about
Nights are getting longer
And the trees are going bare.

Watch out, watch out
Winter is about
Biting your toes
And nipping your nose.

**Laura Davidson  (10)**
**St Thomas' Primary School, Riddrie**


# A Lawyer

I saw you with a wig on your head
I heard you putting your case in a logical way
But remember the ethical aspect of your profession
Justice is nothing but the truth
You may be a good judge on Earth
But the best judge is waiting for you and I,
In Heaven.

**Moyo Adenmosun  (9)**
**St Thomas' Primary School, Riddrie**

# My Little Friend

A little bird sitting on a tree
He loves to sing a song to me
I put out food for him each day
Hoping he will want to stay.
I know that he has lots of friends
But I will love him to the end.

**Caitlin McKenzie  (10)**
**St Thomas' Primary School, Riddrie**


# Flowers

Flowers will die
The sun will set
But you're a friend I won't forget.
Your name is Precious, it will never grow old
It's engraved in my heart with letters of
       *Gold!*

**Katrina Hughes  (10)**
**St Thomas' Primary School, Riddrie**